PINK

Where Ignorance and Cowardice Collide

Nate Schnackenberg

Bellwether SD

Bellwether SD
Colorado Springs, CO

Copyright © 2014 Nathan Schnackenberg

All rights reserved. Published 2014

ISBN:0692205101
ISBN-13:9780692205105

Cover Illustration and Design by Christopher Campion

DEDICATION

To the millions who have died in the Christian IDP camp of secular humanism…

To the men and women pursuing the mountain.

CONTENTS

	Acknowledgments	8
	Prologue	10
1	A Tall Lanky Clown	24
2	Identifying PINK	36
3	Seduction	43
4	Masculine Courage	58
5	Feminine Sagacity	67
6	You're Not Special	78
7	Submission	88
8	The Horizontal Hierarchy	101
9	The Vertical Hierarchy	118
10	New Eyes	131
11	Addiction	139
12	Carnage on the Home Front	150
13	Carnage on the Inside	165

14	Isolating in Shame	185
15	The Mansion	197
16	When It Gets Physical	210
17	Ripped off the Hooks	222
18	The Voice of the Beast	230
19	Birthright, Inheritance, and Destiny	241

ACKNOWLEDGMENTS

Chuck Border, for flushing the book to illuminate the message. Chris Campion, for your work on the cover. Val Schnackenberg, for editing and wisdom.

Prologue

Nearly 2 million people were relieved to stop, make camp, and rest a while. They had been walking for weeks. The road was arduous, jagged, and dangerous. The weather was blistering by day, frigid by night. The desert had already claimed nearly 100,000 of the weakest among them, mostly elderly and children too young to cope with the harsh elements. The people were trying to put on a good face, but it was difficult. A spirit of desperation was overtaking the young nation.

Throughout the encampment men, women and children survived by pushing aside the grief and sorrow they felt for the loss of so many. They had no time for grief; they hadn't even the time to properly bury the dead. Life had been reduced to a minute by minute, day by day slugfest just to breathe.

It wasn't supposed to be like this. It wasn't supposed to be this hard. The promise had been put forth with imagery of a land flowing with milk and honey. This place was a desolate wasteland, a harsh and unrelenting desert scape as far as the eyes could see. Fat livestock, an abundance of food and drink, a sense of safety and security; what happened to *that* promise? Had they been duped? Had they unwittingly followed a lunatic into a mass grave?

That lunatic is Moses, the people are the Israelites, and their location is the Sinai Peninsula circa 1350 BCE. These disheveled people are about to become the center of a universal struggle between the forces of good and evil.

They make camp in a large semi-fertile valley; northwest of the Gidi Pass, due north of the Buruk River, east of Mount Sinai. Vegetation grows in patches along the banks of the watercourse that snakes lazily to the southeast. Daily, the young boys and teenagers escort the sheep and goats to the river's edge to feed, but nobody is worried about overgrazing. They own precious few livestock. These are peasants, former slaves. The people who call themselves the Israelites are the poorest of the poor.

In the distance everyone can see the top two-thirds of the mountain Sinai. It is quite a sight. Day and night the mountain is a whirling inferno, though no vegetation grows on its slopes. The fire is consuming a different sort of fuel, and is putting out a thick black smoke that rises miles into the sky. Their leader has said that the fire burns because the mountain is the dwelling place of God. The masses have no reason to disagree.

Occasionally they hear a bone shaking *crack*, like the sound that blisters seconds before an earthquake. It splinters across the valley with frightening ferocity. Most of the people have come to believe that this thunderous crack is indeed the very voice of God.

The people have been camped now for over a month. This valley is better than the desert road; to this extent nearly everyone agrees. But it is a far cry from the Promised Land, and certainly not a place worthy to be called home. Fierce disputes are commonplace among the elder men as they argue about whether or not the encampment is better than slavery in the land of Egypt. It has become a running quarrel.

Rumor has now spread through the camp that Moses had been spotted walking east, toward them, coming from the mountain. He'd been gone for a long time, and the people were beginning to wonder if he'd ever return. The rumor said he was carrying something in his arms.

Emotionally charged, the nation's elders set out to meet him halfway. There was no uniform consensus on what they would ask for, but they all psychologically chambered their demands nevertheless. Once they came to within shouting distance they started pelting him with relentless fervor. They accosted him with requests and ultimatums; everyone wanted some change to the status quo. Some were convinced that the best course of action was to return to Egypt. Others said that the valley was cursed, and pled with him to move the people further north. Still others demanded the nation split into smaller, more manageable groups and be allowed to fend for themselves.

As the people clamored and shouted, the group worked its way back to the encampment. Moses, who struggled as an orator, was considering how best to respond when in the distance he saw a pedestal, and on the pedestal a golden calf. His peripheral vision blurred as the voices of the elders faded into a muffled drone. He could not take his eyes off it. Something, or *someone*, had infiltrated the camp and left a mark. A calling-card.

His heart began to gallop as his eyes searched the faces of his countrymen.

Which of you did this? He thought, *which one of you let this evil into our camp?*

The more they shouted the less he heard. All of their contorted faces looked the same; they were each driven to outrage and frustration. Nobody was thinking clearly, for a spirit of chaos was descending on them from another world. Even the voice of God cracking in the distance seemed withdrawn.

"Let me take rest," Moses put his hands up to quiet the people. "Dear brothers, let me take rest. I have received our orders from the living God who dwells in the mountain and you will be pleased, but first let me rest a little."

Reluctantly, the elders let him depart to the area of the camp where the Levites had pitched their tents. These were his people, for Levi son of Jacob, son of Isaac, son of Abraham was Moses's great-grandfather. In the company of his family, he was finally able to recline and think through the madness.

He sat near the fire as they told the story of how the golden calf had come into existence. "The people were frustrated," one of the men said, "they did not know whether you were dead or alive, and they started …"

"That doesn't matter," Moses waved with defiance, "frustration never gave anyone permission to defy truth."

The crackle of the fire sent tiny embers into the dark night. Moses adjusted a thick sheepskin draped over his shoulders and shook his head in thoughtful disbelief. *Why did they so quickly abandon their roots and betray me like this?*

He bit his lip in shame. *No, why did they betray You, not me…*

Normally the camp turns down for bed when the sun sets because fire fuel can be hard to come by. Wood is nearly nonexistent, so dried animal waste is the preferred fuel choice whenever the people need a fire for warmth or for cooking. If they had to move around after sundown, they'd burn a flame using clay-made handheld oil lamps. But the lamps cast no heat, so as the cold air of nightfall descends on the camp most are quick to bundle up and hibernate until dawn.

On this night however, sleep evades the people. They are anxious. Small yellow fires dot the valley floor as the Israelites wait for word on when Moses is going to address them.

"What do you want to do?"

Pink

The question pulled Moses from a blank stare. A dozen Levites gazed back at him as shadows danced across their expressions, obstructing their individual perspectives. This moment was a clear picture of the *fog of war*.

War, Moses thought, *this was a journey to the Promised Land of peace, and now suddenly this nation has been besieged by a new war. I don't know what to do…*

He glanced to his right and saw the mountain ablaze under the manifest glory of the living God. Beneath the thick black smoke, bright amber and reddish orange fire lit the sky and mountain with intensity. The spectacle was breathtaking.

"I'll tell you what we're not gonna do," Moses said in almost a whisper. "We will not defy God."

He nodded in the direction of Mount Sinai and his countrymen turned and looked. With their gaze firmly fixed on the mountain, the fog of war lifted and Moses knew what had to be done.

"I'm going to the center square." Moses said, "Get the men, tell them to get their weapons, and tell them that tonight they exact justice on behalf of the living God."

The tablets on which God inscribed 10 commandments in tote, Moses made his way to the center of the encampment; to the gathering place. Rumor spread like a brush fire. The men and elders hustled ahead, hoping to stake claim to preferable vantage points. Women and children were told to stay back so the council could meet, for the gathering place was only large enough for a few hundred.

As Moses zigzagged his way through the encampment women, children and young men came to the threshold of their tents just to get a glimpse of the one who had led them out of Egypt. Love him or hate him, his celebrity was a powerful draw. On this night he carried two huge tablets in his arms and was flanked by two dozen armed Levites. Something was about to happen.

At the gathering place the elders took their seats as Moses raised his hand, beckoning silence. He asked two of his men to fetch the pedestal and golden calf. Working up his courage and resisting his stammer, Moses hoisted the tablets into the air and began.

"The living God inscribed these two tablets with 10 commands, and told me to bring them to you." On this night,

Moses decided to start at number ten and work his way back to the first commandment. It seemed more fitting this way.

"You shall not covet your neighbor's home, you shall not bear false witness, you shall not steal, you shall not commit adultery, you shall not murder, you shall honor your father and your mother, you shall keep the Sabbath day holy, and you shall not take the name of the Lord your God in vain."

He paused and swallowed, trying to remove the lump from his throat. The people were listening intently; the camp was quiet and still.

"You shall not make for yourself a carved image of God, and you shall have no other gods before Me. So commands the living God in the mountain."

Tears welled as he pushed back against raw emotion that abruptly crashed along the banks of his subconscious. His gaze dipped from the people and settled on the graven image that perched before him. He noticed its ornamental, gaudy, shimmering brilliance. He swallowed again, fighting the lump that would not leave. The people waited as if collectively holding their breath. They knew that those last two commandments were a direct indictment on their recent behavior. What was Moses going to do about it? The unease was thick as the Levite warriors slid their hands onto the hilts of their swords.

"You," Moses said with surprising volume and force, "shall have no other gods before me!"

With that declaration he smashed the tablets down on the head of the graven image and everything shattered with a loud *bang* and a flash of light. The golden image, the tablets, everything broke into a billion pieces. Then turning to his men he commanded, "Friend, relative, family member. Whether old or young, man or woman, destroy every person who had anything to do with the creation of the graven image."

On command the Levite warriors jumped into the unarmed crowd and began working their way through the encampment in groups of 4. They killed every man, woman and youth known to be responsible for the idolatry. Amid loud and shameless pleas for mercy they were cut down, one by one, their carcasses piled in a heap outside the perimeter of the camp. By the time the sun crested the eastern horizon, the dead exceeded 3,000 and the judgment was nearly complete.

The sounds of wailing and bitter lamentation echoed throughout the encampment. Women screamed and children cried as the young men readied themselves for a fight. Relatives of the deceased hurled insults and threats at the Levites, and Moses in particular. The masses were verging on outright revolt; the young nation of Israel stood on the brink of civil war.

"You need to do something," one of his henchmen pled.

"Gather the elders," Moses replied. "I want to speak with them outside the eastern gate."

"What elders? We just massacred the lot of them!"

"Then tell the people," Moses shoved his henchmen, "to elect a new ones. Wiser ones. Tell the newly elected to meet me at the gate at sundown. Go quickly."

As the sun dipped toward the west, one by one, the newly elected elders of the people of Israel emerged from the encampment. This time they were not going to be caught off-guard, and they arrived with an armed contingent of their own. They poured out of the encampment and overwhelmed the area around Moses. Their response was overkill, for Moses had not even brought his chief deputy, Aaron. If the people meant to kill him they'd make swift work of it because even Moses was unarmed.

Defensively, the elders took their seats. For the moment, they appeared tentatively willing to hear him out…

* * * * * * * * * *

Obviously, this is an embellished story based on an event in Scripture. I don't know the details of how this actually played out, but in my mind I believe it could have gone something like this. We'll never know.

The people of Moses's era were very much the same as the people in this generation. Confounded by difficult circumstances, they justified all sorts of beliefs and behaviors in an attempt to manufacture a sense of purpose, safety and security. We do the same. It's human nature. When real frustrations abound, it's easy to complain and fret our way straight into a dangerous underworld; a shadowy world full of smoke and mirrors. It's a place that's foreign to our earthly experience because it is not governed by the laws of nature, but by spiritual forces of good and evil.

The manifestation of that evil is not what we might suspect. It is not a ravenous wolf, a dangerous bear, or a mythical dragon breathing fire. In the underworld, evil manifests more like an eccentric merry-andrew, a goofy clownish figure whose primary tactics revolve around mind games, trickery and sleight of hand. Not overt, this character slithers through the minds of people, concocting imaginative accusations and building indictments based entirely on circumstance and emotion. This clown is a master of deception. We are the masterfully deceived.

The encampment built by the Israelites in the valley near Mount Sinai might have been called, the *Israeli Displaced People's* camp. At the time of its inception, it housed an initial settlement of 2 million people according to best estimates. Today the population of that camp has ballooned to over 2 billion.

Though the acronym remains the same, IDP camp now stands for *Internally Displaced People* - for we are the men and women of Christianity, abiding in our country of origin but displaced and homeless by virtue of our graven images and outright rejection of the living God. We have learned to be comfortable in these surroundings, amid the dust and filth of livestock living. Somewhere along our journey, we lost the will to dream about the Promised Land, for this mucky, swarming encampment has become all we know. It's become our home.

At the center of this sprawling metropolis there is a small pedestal and on it, a golden calf. Millions of people pass by it every day but the clown's calling card is no longer offensive. It's hardly even recognized for what it is.

Join me as we journey beneath the Pink streets of tent-city - the Christian IDP camp of our modern era - where the 'faithful' come to die…

Chapter 1 – A Tall, Lanky Clown

The vision opened with a close-up of a huge, ugly, angry looking dog. More than a dog, this creature was a beast with broad shoulders and thick scars all over its face. Salivating, it growled and barked and snipped maniacally as though cursed with rabies. The beast was lunging and scraping its way toward something, but its movement was restricted.

The vision panned out to illuminate the restriction. The beast was chained to a heavy brick and metal doghouse. With every heave and lunge, it pulled the doghouse along the slick concrete floor of a massive warehouse, but the forward momentum was slow. Hurling all his weight into the effort, each lunge only yielded a fraction of an inch.

Around the beast's neck was a collar and pendant.

The vision panned out further and revealed that the beast was just one in a circle of other crazed and angry creatures, all behaving similarly. Each was chained to something that inhibited forward movement, and each had a collar and pendant. The sharp echo of barks, snarls, and growls bounced between the stone walls of the warehouse. Every creature was violently trying to get to the middle of the circle.

Next the vision focused on what looked like a deranged clown, standing in the middle of the ring of beasts. He was tall and lanky, his face paint was smudged, and his clothes were too small for his frame. His posture stooped at the shoulders. He watched the beasts with a sinister grin as they inched closer.

In his right hand he held onto a dainty little leash, barely thicker than string. The leash was loosely draped around the neck of a sheep that sat, downcast and pitiful at the clown's feet. The sheep was bloody and bruised. Its aura screamed of hopelessness and dejection. Every time the clown moved, the sheep twitched as though afraid it might receive a beating.

The clown's cocky demeanor changed as the beasts inched to within a few feet of him. His ominous facial expressions turned to agitation as he withdrew a thick metal chain. It had had two large rusty meat hooks affixed to one end. Perturbed by the encroaching beasts, the clown moved quickly and rammed the rusty hooks into the sheep's back. The sheep squealed with pain; a high pitch that echoed over the sound of angry barks.

The clown then tossed the other end of the chain over a banister along the ceiling. The sheep's wail turned into a whimper as the blood squirting from her back covered her pale wool in a pinkish hue. The clown giggled like a school girl and stopped what he was doing momentarily, just to savor the sheep's pain. After mocking the wounded ewe, he tugged on the free end of the chain and hoisted the sheep up into the air by the hooks. She kicked and jerked and tried to free herself from the hooks, but her effort was in vain.

The clown then anchored the free end of the chain and climbed up into the rafters to perch, safely out of the reach of the invading beasts. There, hidden by partial shadow he looked psychotic. His nostrils flared and he took irregular breaths. Occasionally he'd blurt a giggle and clap his hands as if he was witnessing the greatest show on earth.

Once they were within reach, the beasts began jumping and snipping at the dangling sheep. More slack was needed so they kept heaving toward the center. Eventually one of them bit down on the sheep's heel and locked its jaw. It flung to and fro in a violent attempt to free the sheep. Another beast then bit onto the leg of the first, and furiously tugged backwards. Working together, the beasts eventually ripped her off the hooks in a grizzly scene of determination.

The beasts then quieted around the unconscious sheep. They took turns licking and dressing her wounds, and eventually the sheep opened her eyes. She was not dead; badly wounded, but not dead. The beasts then took up defensive postures around her. The clown was no longer sitting in the banisters but assuredly they knew, he'd always be trolling about.

* * * * * * * * * *

The sheep in this vision represented the Church, and the Lord likened that reference to John 10 in the Bible. The beasts represented an awakening and resurgence of truth. The doghouse and other movement inhibitors represented God's will and timing while the warehouse was representative of His authority and permission. The collars and pendants represented ownership and unique calling; they assured that each beast had an owner and each beast had been trained for a specific function. The dogs/beasts each looked unique, but their call of duty was very similar.

The Clown was a strange, mysterious looking creature. His arms and legs were long and thin, and his clothing was too small for his frame. He did not possess the classical big nose or big red shoes; rather, his facial features were sharp and his demeanor was anything but funny. He looked old and calloused, as if his age spanned the centuries. Deep wrinkles carved up his face and hatred lived in his black eyes. The smudged makeup gave him a deranged and psychotic quality. In every sense of the word his appearance was *creepy*.

The clown stands as a mockery to humanity. If his expressions could speak he'd have said, "Look here. If I smudge a little makeup on my face like this, and put on a suit, and ruffle my hair up like this, you idiots can't identify me as the fraudulent, vile creature that I am."

The clown is a representation of Satan's spiritual warfare tactics. Satan's mission is to steal, kill and destroy life. But if he simply steals, kills, and tries to destroy us in explicit combat, would he not become the object of our collective hatred? If he were overt, his methods would backfire on his purpose. This is why the tactics of the enemy were symbolized by a clown instead of something more scary and overt.

Spiritual attack is sleight-of-hand, meant to confuse and befuddle. Spiritual warfare is a mind game. The clown's deceit is evidenced by challenging circumstances and emotional upheaval, and he uses these things to convince us of his lies. Spiritual attack does not seek to kill and maim in the open, it seeks to numb and injure, and ultimately steal away the true identity of the Lord's beloved.

Using trickery, sleight of hand, manipulation, mind games and other sneaky tactics, the clown seeks to confuse and complicate simple truth. He pretends to be a friendly Rhodes Scholar; a professor of logic. He goes to great lengths to reason with us. He is masterful at pushing a covert agenda. He is the embodiment of the dark arts, an ancient wizard of malice and pure evil dressed up to look like an entertainer of children.

It's time to throw away our preconceived notions of a horned devil engulfed in flames. Satan is smoke and mirrors. Satan is deception. Satan is not a fire-breathing dragon; he is a whimsical creature adept at mind control.

For generations he has enjoyed a golden age of prosperity, but he has come to his zenith point and is poised for a dramatic decline. God is giving new revelation and insight, and raising up authentic leaders in a kingdom parched for truth. The most courageous among us hold chalices fit for new wine, and we are beginning to wake up to the reality of the world in decay.

The Sheep represented the worldwide Christian church. Contained within her are individuals of dynamic faith as well as the outright misguided, and every fence squatter in between. The sheep was portrayed as a tired, beat-up, cowardly animal that had very little fight left in her. She wore a collar and leash, presumably because she showed more aggression and defiance toward the clown at other points in history past. But in this vision, the collar and leash were ceremonial at best as she was fully beholden to the clown's will.

The symbolism was less a dig at the worldwide church for being a cowardly entity, and more of an acknowledgement of how hard it has become for men and women of faith to simply breathe. Every fundamental tenant of Christian faith appears to be under assault. It's hard to live according to faith because fundamental Christian truth has become so offensive and misunderstood. Because authentic truth has been used as a bargaining chip, the believing community no longer has claim to it and the kingdom as a whole has fallen into obscurity and division.

If the vision began and ended with the clown's hypnotic power over the sheep, I wouldn't have bothered writing this book. But that wasn't the extent of the message. Quite the contrary.

Enter, the Beast.

The Beasts represent an outcry of fury from a distant place. Like the Prophets of old who laid claim to truth with radical conviction, the beasts bring a message that is uniformly despised both in the world and in the church. Rugged and raw, they are offensive in appearance, message and mannerism. The quintessential bull in a china shop, nobody likes the beast. Not even the sheep.

The beasts frighten the church because they've got enough fire in their bellies to turn over tables and upset the status quo. They are an enigma, however, because though they are the counterbalance to the clown's deceit, their methods buck the inbred absolutes of political correctness, gentleness, tepidness and cowardice found all over the pink church. Indeed, truth has become such a foreign concept that though the beasts behave according to it, theirs is a foreign presentation to the majority who live in the Christian encampment.

The beast has always existed, but authentic truth-bearers of generations past have been dispatched to the remote hills of our faith. The beasts do not represent a new breed of Christian that shall suddenly arise; they represent an ancient class that shall suddenly *revive*. They represent the return of the spirit of Elijah. The beasts are an authentic and ancient order, commissioned to take back the mantle of truth from a kingdom that has lost its way.

The beast's behavior is a problem for the sheep. The beast intends to reverse alliances that the church has made with the world about how the kingdom of God expresses itself. About what the kingdom believes, and why it's on this dusty planet to begin with. As they reverse these alliances, chaos and warfare will break out.

As the beasts lay hold of authentic truth, those who abide in Christendom will be called *Bigot*! And *Hater*! As the secular world hurls insults, inevitably, the sheep will do what she does best and bow to the pressures of conformity. What else can she do? She has no moral authority anymore, for she has sold it for the right to worship at the neck of a golden calf. As a nation she has chosen safety in man and separation from God.

The clown has had a jolly good time oppressing the so-called 'faithful' these past many generations. He's got the Christian church community so whipped and irrelevant that many within the church have forgotten their faith altogether. They wouldn't know truth of it flopped out of the sky and landed on their face. That's why the rescue can't come from within, and why the rescue will come from elsewhere; the ostracized hill-dwellers of old. God has shielded them for a time and a place such as this, and he will unloose them on pink Christianity in the years to come.

Truth is this: As long as the sheep coexists with the spirit of progressive humanism and remains in subservience to the spiritual forces wielded by the clown, the sheep – *Church* – will hate the beast. Only after the sheep has become completely irrelevant and gets ripped off those rusty hooks will she begin to transform into what she's destined to be; the beautiful, spotless bride of Christ.

* * * * * * * * * *

This book may offend the reader at times. I don't know how to get around this because I cannot in good conscience abide by the rules that have been set forth by the clown, adopted and endorsed by the pink sheep. I can't. I'm not going to adjust the message for the sake of reader sensitivity. Upfront, it's important that the reader understand that this book is not for everybody, and it may be unsuitable for *you*.

Pink

This book is about the war, and I'm going to paint vivid pictures of what that war looks like. I promise to reintroduce *truth*, and know that truth is a wildly offensive concept to the world at large. Those who are familiar with truth will have no problem with this book.

This book is about war. This book comes to you from the resurgence of the beasts. If you've not known truth before, may this book serve as the first echo of a distant bark, and may your passions ignite anew.

Chapter 2 – Identifying PINK

Pink is a watered down red. If red represents a pure heart, pink is representative of a heart that's spliced with ulterior motive. Red stands alongside wisdom while pink aligns with knowledge. Red centers on the supremacy of God, while pink centers on the supremacy of man. Red counsels with empathy, pink with sympathy. Red is courage, pink is cowardice.

The color of the blood that poured onto the rocks of Calvary was red. That blood did away with the law and exchanged it for intimacy. Pink is the color of the law that strangles and divides; red is the color that unites. Pink is found in feigned public piousness; red is found in transparent humility. Red feels uncomfortable as it liberates us to freedom. Pink feels uncomfortable as it condemns us to prison.

Pink Christianity is a term derived in part by the blood-splattered wool of the sheep from the previous chapter. Pink Christianity is *compromise everything, stand for nothing and fight for less Christianity*. Pink Christianity is "give me my salvation so long as you don't dare touch my house, health insurance, and annual vacation in the Bahamas."

Pink

Pink messaging is all over the church. Things like *the money code, get rich fast* message. Or the, *every good person goes to heaven* message. One of my personal favorites is the, *God doesn't do supernatural things anymore* message. Or how about the *don't judge if you don't want to be judged* message? What these and countless others have in common is that they value vanity over authenticity, humanity over divinity. They elevate the human's temporal circumstance while downgrading the Omni-God.

Authentic truth cannot be spliced with anything lest it become completely false. Truth is therefore singular, and lies are *every single counterfeit* no matter how small the additive. The pure red of truth turns pink when, though we purport to live by a fundamental set of values, we compromise them because circumstances change. Pink shows up when we let our kids get away with arguing their way out of a consequence for bad behavior. It invades when we lack a sense of greater purpose, and choose to live by a self-centered code of ethics.

The brick-and-mortar church is not the problem. Pink is the color that's brought in by the people who gather. Pink attitudes are more prevalent if the group is led by someone speaking from behind a pink pulpit, but ultimate responsibility for the color of *your* faith is *yours and yours alone.*

In the spring of 2008 I sat in the pew one Sunday morning and listened to an ordained pastor deliver a short message. The "Senior Pastor" was out of town so the replacement speaker - who appeared to draw the short straw - spoke on a few passages from the book of Joel chapter 2.

The book of Joel encourages preparedness, and warns of a great and terrible army that shall one day be unloosed upon earth, among other things. To any sane human being this is a *heavy* story. The depictions are gritty, frightening and wildly convicting. It evokes images of violence and orients the reader's heart toward a God of justice.

Midway through the message the speaker said something like, "You know, when I was a youth, I believed this book represented something of a 'call to arms'. Then I grew up and realized that God just wants to love our hearts…"

He went on to talk about how loving and caring and empathetic God is.

He wasn't wrong about that, and I can appreciate messages that illuminate the truth about our loving God. But do you see the PINK in his message? The book of Joel chapter

2 is a candidly written, gruesome, gritty prophecy of a hellish season for all who live to see it. It's not a touchy-feely message about how God just wants to love human hearts. Teach the insatiable desires of God out of books like Song of Solomon all day long, but don't pretend to have wisdom amid such an abject lack of courage. It's embarrassing.

Every Sunday "pastors" all over the world pander to congregations. They do so out of ignorance, fear, and in the worst cases, nefarious alignment with the clown. Pink messaging has systematically hijacked a kingdom birthed in truth, and turned a red messages into a melting pot of putrid pink gunk.

Pink happens when we willfully dilute what's real and pimp falsities in order to appease the sensibilities of the lost and insecure. Pink Christians forever take red elements of God's character and reengineer them for the sake of appeasement. They live as though they're on an eternal quest to find their lost baby blanket. They yearn for the fluffy emotional coddling that comes by way of a zero-sum message. They are so addicted to their false sense of identity that they do anything and everything, even *make crooked the straight path of righteousness,* to manufacture a guilt-free and judgment-free message.

Pink Christianity is the result of the clown's success in the lives of individuals. He couldn't steal the entire kingdom at once so he's been patient, hijacking the kingdom one individual at a time. The clown talks us into believing that our identity is insecure. He talks us into false imagery about the true nature of God. He's a fear monger who preys on the scared. Then, from a place of insecurity and terror we naturally reach for pink stuff because red seems too harsh.

Pink eases the coarseness of life's challenges by telling us that everything goes and nothing counts. Pink faith is a cafeteria, a hodgepodge of soothing balms and Band-Aids effective at easing the pain of guilt and shame. It tells us to mirror the actions of a pacifist God who is unengaged and uninterested in the plight of humanity. We bury our heads in the sand and keep to being "good people" in life so that our God in heaven – who, according to pop-pink-lore prefers to never judge - will not judge us in the end.

Pink is everywhere but it's hard to admit to in our own lives. Most of us choose to live in isolation, and hide our darkest traits from those around us. The truth about our decaying nature is often a point of insecurity, and not something we like sharing with the community. If someone has the audacity to push on one of these hidden characteristics, we tend to explode with outrage, "How dare you judge me? Look at yourself!"

Calm down, kid. Take a deep breath. We are all equally corrupt. Your secrets are no different than mine, so maybe it's time for a different response. Maybe it's time to abandon those insecurities and start living as though we belong to the King.

The pink behave as though desperate to avoid confrontation, but all they ever experience *is* confrontation. The world hates the pink Christian for his/her firm-tentative, noncommittal, non-confrontational endorsement of Christ, so conflict reigns. Likewise, God wishes He could hock the pink from His mouth because their lukewarm pacifism is like vomit. (Revelation 3:16). In this way, conflict reigns on the home front as well. It is no wonder the sheep from the previous vision was so downcast and dejected. She can't win. She never wins.

Pink. It's a god-awful color.

Chapter 3 – Seduction

The faceless man stretched his hand toward the goddess and noticed a quiver in his wrist. His fingers twitched as they ran along the strap of her gown. Her skin was perfect and smooth. His breath came in hushed gasps as he tried to keep quiet. He dare not wake his wife or kids.

Mesmerized by her full lips, deep dark eyes and long neck, he trembled and inched a little closer. She ran her manicured fingernails along his forearm, tantalizing his senses and luring him further into a state of seductive longing. Cold musty air blew up the staircase, grabbing her alluring scent and wafting it into him. He loved the smell of her. She bit her lip shyly and took another step backward, beckoning him with tempting flirtation to follow her down into the basement.

Her nightgown was almost transparent. He eyeballed her closely as the silky material shuffled and bent around her flawless curves. She took another step backward and he followed, slowly, reluctantly.

The staircase was made of wooden planks that creaked

softly as they advanced. A candle lantern hung from the wall halfway down. In the soft glow his eyes locked with hers. She begged and teased him with her long dark eyelashes, toying with his every emotion.

"Come on," she licked her lips, "Let me take you there again. Let me make your dreams come true."

She took another step back. He followed, but something suddenly tugged at his attention. He glanced up the staircase and saw the cracked door leading into the kitchen. Had somebody woken up? Was it one of his kids, or his wife?

A pang of guilt shot through his gut and he considered retreating. On cue, another blast of stale air came from below, as though competing for his mind. He turned back to the goddess and hesitated. Fear and shame fluttered around his midsection as he pulled his hands away from her and looked back at the kitchen.

He'd been to this basement - more like a dungeon – before. He'd enjoyed the waters of pure ecstasy with the goddess many times prior. She was good to him. She was discrete. She let him do the things of fantasy and always whispered the things he wanted to hear.

But he loved his wife and two kids, and being with the goddess was, at some level, a betrayal to his friends and family. He felt guilty for wanting the goddess. He felt shame and regret for how many times he'd been with the goddess.

Countless times, he thought.

Lust and longing fought hard against shame and guilt and the more each tugged at his heart, the more his knees felt weak. He looked back at the goddess, mired in indecision.

Normally when he fought the urge to flee, the goddess would step closer to him, rub her body against his and beg him not to go. She'd kiss his neck and whisper sweet promises about how good she'd make him feel. She'd caress his face and neck with her long fingers. She'd tickle his ear with her moist tongue. Eventually, inevitably, he'd follow her into the darkness have his way with her.

But this time something was different. She stared at him, completely indifferent toward his struggle. With a coy smile, she leaned against the wall and dug at the cuticles in her fingers and waited patiently.

Pink

"You know you're going to follow me." Her flat tone caught him off-guard, "so follow. Your resistance is fakery. I know what you want, and I always give you what you want. If it's not good enough for you then maybe you should leave…"

"Now hold on just a…" He started, ashamed and angry she so easily mocked his struggle.

"No," she interrupted, "You know I'm right, so drop the theatrics and be a big boy, or go away."

She was right, his struggle was nothing but a weak show of will rooted in guilt and shame, and it had no chance of pulling him out of the dungeon. He didn't like this new version of her. At least when she begged he felt like they were in it together, and her investment helped alleviate his guilt. He didn't like having to go at this alone. It made him feel sick to the stomach.

She smiled, and as she did her already breathtaking features bulged, pulling the gown tight around her torso. He lost his breath and stumbled forward but she caught him and pulled him in tight. She could feel his heart beating wildly as he rested against her, lost again in the euphoria of lust. As they embraced she rolled her eyes with contempt.

The basement ceiling was so low that he had to stoop slightly. The floor was a single slab of cold concrete, and a few dim candle lanterns cast a sinister hue. The musty smell was strong. The basement was empty except for a small cot made of metal in the corner. On it was a thin stained mattress. The memories of passion atop that bed flooded into his mind as his heart skipped.

He started walking toward the cot but she gripped his hand tight and refused to budge. He turned and looked at her, puzzled.

"If you let me, I'll take you places you've never even dreamed of going." She said, her eyes now harder, fixed on his. She eased forward and wrapped her slender arms around his midsection and nibbled on his neck. There was an allure to what she proposed, but something seemed *off*.

His heart thumped like a bass drum as his hands began to explore. Then suddenly she stepped back and tugged his shirt, inching him toward the far wall, away from the cot. He followed her as though sleepwalking, caught in a high that dismissed his better judgment. Her fingers walked down his arms until they reached his wrists where she squeezed tight.

She was strong; her tight grip surprised him. Though something was not right, he couldn't shake the buzz. He lacked the strength to focus on what was going on around him. One step after the other he blindly followed where she led.

Through blurred vision he could see a curve on her mouth, but not the curve of a temptress. It was not seductive at all. It was malevolent. It was the smile of perpetration, as though she intended to devour him like a starved animal to a hunk of rotting meat. It was that curve upon her lips that began the awakening in him. He blinked, shook his head, and then opened his eyes wide as terror gripped his every nerve.

Where is she taking me?

The musty smell was powerful and acrid on this side of the basement. Rot hung in the cold air, but where was the smell coming from? He tugged and fought against her grip but she would not let go. Her face expression didn't even change as she methodically walked backward, leading him toward an unidentified danger that horrified him. He jerked and turned with all his might, so hard that he felt a bone pop in his left wrist. He tried to let out a scream, but couldn't find the breath. Something in the air swallowed his voice. Pain pumped toward his temples.

What's happening? And I gonna die?

They reached an archway in the wall and the goddess suddenly stopped moving. She let the hard smile leave her face. Her chest was now almost flat, her curves mostly gone. She stood before him as a woman still, but much older. He stopped struggling to free himself as his eyes fixated on the arched opening in the wall behind her. Something ancient and terrible lived past that opening. He could feel it. He was more frightened than he had ever been before.

"Won't you come in with me?" she asked, her voice now low and dark.

"I will not," he said, shaking his head. A tear formed at the corner of his eye, "I cannot. I cannot go there with you goddess. Please, I have a wife. I have kids. I don't even want to go back to the cot. I just want out."

"It's too late." A new, powerfully demented voice rose up from behind the arched opening. The faceless man froze with terror.

Pink

The old woman then arched herself backward, pulling him toward the gateway. First the crown of her head touched the opening and disappeared into the blackness that seemed to swallow light. Then her face and neck entered and disappeared behind the dark gateway. As she arched the man began falling forward.

He fought wildly, screaming and begging her to let him go. The pain in his wrist was numbed by the terror in his heart. When only her forearms remained outside the arch, she suddenly lunged forward, back out of the hole. His talking momentum sent him to the ground, flat on his back. She landed on him and straddled his torso.

The creature that emerged from that gateway had the forearms of an old woman, but the rest of it was a hideous mess of rotting flesh, ligaments and bones. It reeked like death. Maggots crawled in and out of its mouth and eyes. It bent down as if to kiss the man when another being climbed out of the gateway. This one was small, the size of a seven year old. It was naked and had hairless, smooth, pasty white skin. Its white eyes stuck like daggers from deep eye sockets. Its thin lips curled sharply downward. The look of it was hideous. Its essence was. Evil.

"Wait Jezebel, this one is mine." It said.

The creature on top of the man snarled and sputtered, then obeyed and let go. As it moved to the side, the naked bald devil mounted and began tearing the faceless man's shirt off. After exposing his chest, the devil opened its mouth wide and took a powerful bite out of his stomach. The man screamed in agony.

The devil continued to devour, ripping out organs and stomach and intestines. He gave some scraps to the creature that had once been so beautiful to his eyes. Eventually, the faceless man stopped fighting as a numbing sensation overtook him in the moments before his death. The sounds of terror faded and everything became slow.

Then this faceless man was given a face. And that face morphed into another. That face morphed into another and another. Slow at first, then faster, the faces morphed from one to another.

The last thing the man saw above the bobbing bald head of the devil was a bright pink flashing neon sign above the archway to hell. It said, "Pornography".

Pink

* * * * * * * * *

That was the account of a vision the Lord gave one of my friends years ago. I too was grossed out when it was first relayed to me. This vision served to convict me of my own propensity to lock the darker sides of my character in the basement.

The wife and kids in this vision represent the greater kingdom. These are the people we live and grow with, our fellowships, friends and families. The dungeon represents the dark place we go to sin. For some it's the office, for others it's the bedroom. Maybe it's a dark alleyway in the city.

The goddess in the vision represents temptation. The portrayal of the goddess pointedly identified the power of sexual temptation, but temptation is more general than that. It could be the temptation to hate, or to malign someone's character, or to steal, or to lie and bear false witness, or to kill, or to check out with drugs, or to partner with the clown, or a host of other things as well.

The cot represented the perception of safety in the context of sin. Some may find safety in manipulating the Lord's grace, where we choose to believe that because God is

Love, He'll ultimately not hold us accountable. It also represented safety in secrecy as well as safety in familiarity and routine.

The devil eating the man's insides represented just that: death from the inside out. Whether it's a pastor falling from the grace of leadership or a husband losing his family, death comes from the inside. It comes from the hidden place where sin is allowed to thrive and fester.

The faceless man fought the temptations with tools such as guilt, shame and regret, but these methods were shown to be ineffective in the vision. They are useless in real life as well. Though ineffective, these are often the tools we use to try and fight through powerful temptations.

For my part, this vision prompted me to take a hard look at the inner self, the darker self, the self that dominates the dungeons of my life. It painted a vivid picture of the reality of my fallen nature, and it mocked my seemingly endless resolve hang on to my pride as I strive to reach a God who's already crossed the great divide.

It was convicting because it identified a terrible alliance I'd made with the clown. I realized that I'd partnered with the lie that says I'm strong enough to manage the reek and rot of death. By partnering with this false assumption, I allowed gangrene to spread through my body and life. A partnership like this works to nullify salvation through grace, and downgrades my reliance on Christ Jesus.

Through the revelation of this alliance, I realized that I lacked the ability to defend myself. Not as though I lacked the will, but I lacked true understanding in the spirit. Like the faceless man, I regularly fought temptations with guilt and guts, but it never seemed to work out in my favor. I came to understand that dealing with temptation in this way was akin to engaging a firefight with a pocket knife. I needed to discover better weaponry; spiritual weaponry. In this way, this vision and others like it prompted me to embark on a journey of discovery about how to better deal with the conniving whispers of deceit in my mind, and the temptations to separate myself from God through sinful indulgence.

In this pursuit I became convinced that when I live devoid of *intentionality* I tend to look at whatever the clown draws my attention to. He's always jumping around and pointing at stuff, and not always "sinful temptations" either. He'll draw my focus onto political issues, current events, circumstantial challenges, relational conflicts, and all sorts of other distractions. All of these diversions are equally damaging because they all serve to derail my intentionality of pursuit. In other words, when I lack intentionality relating to my pursuit of Christ, I become defenseless against the clown's distractions in my day-to-day life. This was a profound realization for me.

It became clear that distraction was and is a fundamental element of the clown's playbook. He uses philosophy packed with mischief. He uses mind games spliced by emotional hot buttons. His sleight-of-hand starts with an attempt to confuse, and if he succeeds the result is spiritual disorientation.

Four years I was the type of individual who regularly got into angry debates about things like removing *in God we trust* from the nation's coinage, or the merits of wealth redistribution, or legalizing drugs, and a host of others. I advocated for what I felt was right to the world around me, and I did this for the purpose of propping up my value system. It wasn't until I began living intentionally that these pursuits were revealed to be distractions. Prior to intentionally pursuing Christ, political talking points were my central focus.

I prefer to live in a country that mirrors my set of values, but my values are not contingent on this nation's agreement. My values don't change when pot is legalized, or when abortion is celebrated, or when new laws extend bar hours, legalize prostitution, or whatever. And contrary to what I used to believe, being front-and-center in the fight to abolish abortion was never an acceptable substitute for being front-and-center in the war to rid myself of the clown's gangrene.

Temporal distractions stifle intentional pursuit of Christ. A life lacking in intentionality is a life wide open to the goddess of temptation. Ritual engagement with the goddess brings only hurt and decay, and may even be fatal. Guilt and shame is to the forces of darkness, what a pocket knife is to an M-16.

These are the truths that became obvious to me as I embarked on my journey of rediscovery. On the foundations of these truths I've been blessed to receive deeper revelations about the true nature of spiritual warfare. But fundamental to the journey is my intentionality. When I lack intentionality, I experience very little forward momentum.

Chapter 4 – Masculine Courage

I've had the reoccurring experience, as many have, of being blasted on the internet and called all sorts of names for having the audacity to voice unpopular opinions. Anonymous guttersnipes have denigrated my character and even threatened my family at times. I used to think ignorance evoked vitriol, but this is not the case. Vitriolic outrage is more often the result of courage than anything else.

Masculine courage is what fuels the beast's forward momentum and pushes him to never give up. It confronts the insecure, and leaves moral outrage in its wake. It boasts loudly and even beats its chest on occasion, and, authentic masculine courage is always quick to apologize to those who became frightened by its ferocity or offended by its presentation. Masculine courage can be a frightening thing, but if tempered by wisdom and grace, it's never a *dangerous* thing.

Masculine courage is the stuff that thrives in trench warfare; be it a football game or on a battlefield. It fights until it dies. It rebuffs hesitancy in a way that wildly offends the insecure. Masculine courage is the thing that a father taps into when his daughter gets abused by bullies on her way home from school. It's what a mother taps into when she does whatever she must to put food on the table for her kids. It's the stuff that gives us the ability to sacrifice ourselves for the ones we love.

This thing is not just for the offense-minded, however. Masculine courage also allows us to take a beating and turn the other cheek. It keeps us from harboring resentment toward bomb throwers who lash out anonymously online. Jesus used it when He boldly admitted to misguided Caiaphas that, indeed, He was the Son of God… and Jesus also used it when He chose not to call down a battalion of heavenly host to smite Rome, though such a response would have been justifiable.

For most of us, masculine courage is a hard nut to crack. One must possess wisdom and a very special grace that comes only by way of the Holy Spirit in order to wield it in truth. Courage without wisdom is immature bravado. Courage without grace renders us susceptible and defenseless to crushing counter attack. Wisdom informs us concerning when and how to be courageous while grace shields us from the clown's counter insurgence.

More challenging still is the fact that even when courage is aligned with wisdom and grace, the pink minded often see it as ostentatious bravado regardless. Put another way, to people who are ensnared in the clown's web of lies, true courage looks just like masculine bravado and is therefore poorly received. The clown is offended by courage, so he talks the easily offended into being morally outraged regardless of the merit of the courageous act. So even if using this weapon in truth and for its intended purpose, we must expect blowback in the physical.

Some may then ask, "if it's a 'damned if you do, damned if you don't' situation, then why use it?"

That's a fantastic question, if you're a person who only sees life in the context of yourself. The antithesis of courage is cowardice, which is rooted in guilt. Only self-righteous people use things like guilt to deal with their interpersonal conflicts in life, just as only self-righteous people would ever question the value and worthiness of masculine courage.

The clown tells us that if we feel bad enough about a situation or wrongdoing, then guilt should be used to pay penance. Though it remains impossible to undo the hurt or remove the spiritual taint, penance makes us *feel* better because we emotionally pay a price for the wrongdoing. Guilt keeps us feeling unworthy, unholy before God, and self-deprecating in a world that demands that the counterbalance to evil be embodied by one who feels fully worthy, holy before God, rooted in a Christ-centric identity.

Guilt excuses perpetrated abuse because how dare we, the guilty and shamed, have the temerity to *judge*? How dare we suppose to exact recompense with clarity when we ourselves fall so short of righteousness? On the surface this argument might seem like wisdom, but ask people suffering at the hand of tyranny whether they're worried about our spotty past? I assure you they aren't. Those suffering simply need help and are waiting for somebody, anybody, to judge evil for what it is and come to the rescue.

This perspective recently played out on the news, when guilty-minded apologists made *moral equivalency* the central issue surrounding the decision of whether or not to stop the Syrian dictator from gassing his own people. According to the guilty-minded cowards, America was unqualified to meddle in the affairs of another country because we have been unjust in our meddling in the past. The argument sounds so wise doesn't it? It goes something like this: "How dare we judge, for we are just as guilty as President Assad!"

What?! When was the last time anyone had to deal with golf ball sized boils on their face because the USA showered them with a dose of poisonous gas? The assertions and arguments of the guilty are lunacy because they are formulated from inside a dungeon so packed full of guilt and shame that nothing else factors in. It's not about innocent women and children dying the most horrific death possible; for the guilty, it's only about mitigating their feelings of guilt and shame.

Guilt is a spiritual weapon that uses the tenants of sympathy to numb and befuddle truth. Masculine courage is a spiritual weapon that uses conviction to energize and clarify it. Guilt whips its own backside and seeks to pay penance. Masculine courage whips the perpetrators' ass and is never afraid to judge wrongdoing. Guilt says that the tenets of *forgive seventy times seven times* (Matt 18:22) is equivalent to 'enable the jerk forever, and keep bailing him out of jail'. Masculine courage on the other hand says the message of Matthew 18:22 is tantamount to "always forgive and retain no sour judgments, but for eternity's sake, let the jerk find his rock-bottom."

Guilt's response to conflict is informed by the emotional imperative. Masculine courage responds to conflict on the basis of inherent truth.

Guilt sympathizes with a teenager who comes home and verbally attacks his mother with a mean and corrosive spirit. Guilt prompts us to justify his verbal abuse on the basis of "problems" that he conveniently refuses to talk about. Guilt has no response, no power, and no authority to administer justice or to lay down a few firm boundaries. This is because the guilty have no right to judge. Guilt tells us that it's okay to quit and give up provided we have a good excuse. Guilt always reinforces failure because it is predicated entirely on the need to *feel* better about disappointment.

Masculine courage, on the other hand, reasons with the angry teen. It empathizes and offers to process the boy's "problems", but makes no adjustment to the expectation of common courtesy and respect in the home. Masculine courage tells the boy how to persevere, fight, and ultimately, *win*. Masculine courage speaks life and success into the struggling teen, and shows him how to face life's hardships face first, dukes up. It never admits an excuse or justifies a corrosive spirit. Ever.

Masculine courage is not a tool we receive at the first *ah-hah* power encounter with God. It's not a tool we find buried in the Bible, although evidence of its existence is everywhere throughout Scripture. Masculine courage is something God bestows on us on the heels of our death to self. This tool is too powerful for the pink. There is too much of a responsibility that comes with it. We can't fake our way into receiving it. We can't pretend to live by the Spirit, because only people who genuinely live by the Spirit actually bear fruit.

Pink Christian men have an interesting ability to deflect certain responsibilities under the guise of pious contemplation. It's the guy whose wife begs him to take her out for a date, and he literally responds to the request by saying something like, "yeah, maybe. I think I should pray about it… We're a little short on money."

Funny thing, she thinks, *you didn't have to pray about going to the football game last week.*

Pink also manifests in guys who clam up and refuse to deal with conflict head-on. A "woe is me" attitude permeates their being on the basis of guilt and shame, and they start living out of a belief that they are "damned if they do, damned if they don't, so why try?"

It's sickening. It's the guy who won't go get a job, or the guy who won't search for a better job, or the guy who sits around and justifies his laziness and apathy on the basis of all his uniquely difficult circumstances. Nothing is more pathetic than a man who lacks the courage to be the hero in his own life's tale. Women despise this because that coward's self-loathing has effectively stolen away *her* fairytale. It's selfish, and its conduct unsuitable for the masculine race.

Another pink manifestation among Christian men is cowardice in the face of his wife's emotional ups and downs. I'm not talking about stifling the emotions; I'm talking about jumping in and being a part of your wife's journey. Cowardly men retreat because female ups and downs can be intimidating and hard to define, but what these guys don't realize is that the roller coaster is just as confusing and hard on the woman experiencing it. By abandoning the situation, all they effectively establish is a propensity to abandon *her*. It's pusillanimity at its worst!

By abandoning emotional situations, we men abandon our responsibility to help discern the root of the emotional struggle. Consequently, we are unable to participate in the rescue. Consequently, the identity of *guilt-stricken coward* is further ingrained in our sense of self, and the cycle repeats. We were designed to be courageous, not cowardly.

Only when we nail our self-righteousness to the cross

does the Lord offer the treasure of courage and say, "Here you go. It will be for you a light in darkness, clarity where there was confusion, hope where apathy reigned. Take this gift and wield it with wisdom and grace, and see to it that you don't stop fighting until you rip that sheep right off the Devil's hook."

Chapter 5 – Feminine Sagacity

Sagacity is the mental ability to understand and discriminate between relations. Put another way, it's being able to define truth by distinguishing and evaluating situations. A sagacious person has the ability to judge right from wrong with wisdom, and possesses the ability to let that judgment inform his/her decisions, actions and behavior.

Boom!

Pink Christians have foregone their responsibility to be sagacious equivalent to the pink church's rejection of masculine courage. Like the pink church's desperate need for a resurgence of masculine courage, so too do we yearn for a resurgence of sagacity.

Masculine courage is not a concept exclusive to men, and feminine sagacity is not an ideal exclusive to women. The gender-specific undertones I affix to each term has to do with my interpretation of powerful gender-specific graces that are evident in men – courage, and women – wisdom.

If God created man to be courageous and women to be sagacious, was it not strategic for the clown to focus his attack on stealing away those attributes? And if so, has the clown not done a valiant job? The clown has been wildly effective at stealing man's courage and exchanging it for timidity, and stealing woman's sagacity and exchanging it for emotional pride. Pink Christian men are often timid cowards; pink Christian women are often belligerently entitled.

I've wondered how the clown managed to be so effective in this fight. He really had to be sneaky because most guys I know like the identity of the hero, and most ladies I know like the identity of wisdom. Nothing upsets a man like being called a *coward* and nothing upsets a woman like being called *emotional*. But this is exactly what we have become in the pink church.

Feminists are a powerful force in this country. In large measure they set the talking points and overall tempo on a national level about an array of morality-based subjects. They lead on issues having to do with reproductive health, marriage, equality (and its many subcategories) and an array of others. Not every woman subscribes to feminine overtures, but very few speak out against it.

Interestingly, when the feminist movement gathered

momentum in the 60s, our culture also experienced a sharp decline of masculine courage. As culture shifted, traditional role responsibilities became confused. To those who championed the cause, it must have seemed like progressive bliss. Men relinquished the full responsibility of household provision while women inherited equal standing in the workplace. At face value it must have seemed like a win-win, but then we fast-forward a generation and begin realizing the cost.

Men have become spiritual eunuchs while women are getting buried under the weight of the responsibilities their 'feminist' counterparts demanded. Hidden within the feminist pursuit was an unforeseen consequence; that is, if told they have no responsibility to marriage and fatherhood, men will often relinquish those responsibilities entirely. To many women this must have been a surprise.

How can he dump on me and the kids like this? How can he so easily go about his life without a care or concern for us?

The reason is because men and women are, regardless of what some say, physiologically different. Many guys don't *attach* at the emotional level that women do. Is that to say guys aren't emotional? No. Guys are emotional, but I don't believe the average guy has the capacity to be emotional at the depth and intensity of the average gal.

As an example, when men fight for custody of children they are fueled by both an emotional *and* intellectual imperative. But when guys don't fight for custody, they abandon that responsibility fully on the basis of intellect. In other words, the intellectual perspective generally trumps the emotional one. Not so for women. Ladies fight this battle on a moral and emotional basis first, and intellect takes a back seat to the more prevalent values of attachment and responsibility.

Men are not going to turn around and suddenly take responsibility for things, just as sure as many women will not give up being the social dominatrix in their relationships. Fathers will continue to be in short supply while welfare systems continue raising an overabundance of single mothers and their offspring. I've come to accept this as our reality. Though culture as a whole is destined to keep its trajectory, individuals are able to change. Though the world has defined a cultural status quo, there is no law that says we must abide by it. Though the pink church is comfortable with the status quo, the citizens of the kingdom don't have to be.

Feminine sagacity is the ability to define truth in the midst of challenging circumstances and emotional upheaval. We're judging all the time, but we often don't do it sagaciously.

It's not OK to get blown this way and that by changing hormones or circumstances. It's not OK to justify petulant outbursts - young ladies - because you're *on your period* or *having a bad hair day*. You still need to be sagacious. It's not good enough to justify throwing caution to the wind and behaving like thugs - young men - because you're confused and feel insecure. You still need to be sagacious.

To some extent, poor behavior in the church is legitimized because it's constantly reinforced in popular culture. Culture applauds women who emasculate men, and denigrates men for doing anything about it. Pop-culture says, "Ladies, take authority and lord it over anyone and everyone according to your will," and simultaneously says, "Gentlemen, relinquish your authority and do what you're told."

The clown's fingerprints are all over this.

To some extent faith enables us - even those of us with a pink hue - to exercise a counterattack against this cultural message. Most believers I know have a healthier understanding than the world does relating to masculine and feminine grace.

But nevertheless, what's gaining momentum within the church is female leadership at the expense of male participation. Nowadays, it seems like the only guys left attending faith-based gatherings are young boys or flaccid dude-bro's. That's because the men are out working on their cars, shooting guns, drinking beer or attending a ballgame. They are somewhere in the company of people who choose not to chastise them for being who they were made to be.

The classical church fellowship has lost just about all appeal to most guys, and that's why 80% of nationwide church attendees are women and children. Who'd want to go to a hostile environment and be ridiculed?

A lack of sagacity fosters a climate that breeds outrage and despair, which opposes the fruit of the Spirit. Guys and gals alike behave poorly when they judge circumstance without sagaciously filtering the data. In this climate we become prone to promiscuity, glorifying wrongs, behaving horribly toward one another, and are constantly seeking justification for our lifestyles.

Alternatively, when we judge circumstances sagaciously a different sort of climate is fostered. Truth is not bent by the changing winds of circumstance or the justification of emotion.

Truth is foundational. It's fundamental. An abundance of sagacity fosters a climate where we encourage one another, see the best in one another, and value ourselves according to the eyes of God, not man.

If a sagacious person judges by filtering data through truth, a pink person judges by filtering data through pride. The opposite of feminine sagacity might therefore be called *prideful justification*.

Prideful justification is self-centered, and judges on the basis of the self's emotional need at that instant. Prideful justification defends lifestyle choices while feminine sagacity defends values. Prideful justification encourages indulgence, while feminine sagacity encourages temperance. Prideful justification says that malicious gossip isn't that bad because the object of the gossip won't ever find out… "And if she does, I can always deny I said it".

Prideful justification is the basis for doing things we want over doing things we ought. Feminine sagacity not only doesn't participate in wrongs, but if it identifies a malicious spirit in and among those who are participating in wrongdoing, it lovingly and directly confronts the spirit. Prideful justification is cowardly and reactive while feminine sagacity is brave and proactive.

Feminine sagacity is loving and firm in how it addresses conflict. Prideful justification is sensitive, sarcastic and back-handed when addressing conflict. Feminine sagacity is evident in a life that is defined by peace. It's unafraid of working through conflicts face-to-face. Prideful justification is evident in a life that is defined by chaos, and avoids addressing conflicts face-to-face.

Feminine sagacity values authentic relationships, and knows that authenticity is attained in vulnerability. Prideful justification values superficiality because it can only thrive among the disingenuous and guarded.

Sagacious people know that their wisdom and discernment is found in Christ. They have a special insight that defies human understanding, and they practice it with ease and grace. Sagacious women are not confronted or bothered by the notion of femininity, submission, maternity, or the like. They are not irritated about their place in the workforce, home, or other societal arenas. They breathe life and pleasure into any setting because they so effortlessly reflect godly wisdom and discernment. They are never defined by insecurity – they don't experience insecurity the way the proud do. Feedback is no longer scary, and they are totally and completely secure in their own skin. These people wear joy like a blanket, and everyone wants to be around them.

Something magical happens when a woman who was designed for sagacious wisdom chooses to embrace it and live by it. The magic is not just in the fact that these ladies live in stark contrast to the insecure flow of feminism throughout society, but it's in the credit they become to their homes, businesses, and social networks. There is nothing more frightening to a person under the yolk of prideful justification then a woman living free of the bondage of insecurity.

Contrarily, ladies who wield prideful justification seek validation by how closely they mirror their behavior to that of a man's, or what shoes they wear, or how promiscuous they are, or what type of jewelry they put through their private parts, or how their hair looks, or what have you. For older ladies it's this constant pursuit of the fountain of youth. Women in this country and those in the pink church spend more on cosmetics in a month than most people earn in a year in the Third World.

Pink Christian ladies attempt to derive value by asserting themselves as the de facto decision-maker in any context. They are always monopolizing conversations, and focus a tremendous amount of energy on making sure their 'works' in life are duly noted and acknowledged by everyone present - so long as those 'works' have nothing to do with traditionally feminine activities, of course.

A re-valuation of feminine sagacity is of paramount importance to the dangling sheep because at some level, the sheep needs to allow the beast to rip her off the rusty hook. Those living under the heavy yolk of prideful justification could never suffer the indignity of having to be rescued! To the extent that courage and sagacity are required for the beast to fulfill its purpose, courage and sagacity are also attributes needed for the sheep.

What's interesting is that a man who wields masculine courage naturally develops a sagacious tendency that endears him to the softer side of humanity. Similarly, women who choose feminine sagacity naturally develop a fiercely courageous side that strikes fear in the clown and its pink minions. This is because one cannot exist without the other, and vice versa. This is what makes courage and sagacity so profound.

Nobody would be able to execute a sagacious judgment

without courage, and a lack of courage would inhibit our strongest attempt to be sagacious in the first place. In this way, the healthy church family promotes and defends the ideals are of sagacity and courage, and embraces the unique designs built into each gender because God knew what he was doing in the first place.

Chapter 6 – You're Not Special

The clown is masterful at taking truth, splicing it with a dab of untruth, and selling the witch's brew as though it were the genuine article. The message of uniformity is a great example.

Though it is not overt, the *You're Not Special* message is all over the pink church. It's evident in the systems of hierarchy, industry and expectations of conformity. In its marriage to the world, the pink church has defined very specific limitations and boundaries pertaining to intimacy, worship and individualism before Christ. Though most pastors don't brazenly say, "You're ordinary and must conform to this fellowship's standard of relationship with God and man," the systems that oversee the pink church subliminally drive this message home at every opportunity.

Why does it matter? It matters because uniformity of thought, behavior, and perspective deadens unique expressions of intimacy, and breeds things like lethargy and apathy. When a group is issued predefined standards of thought and behavior, individuals inherit no responsibility for their own pursuits of identity in Christ. This quiet unassuming message is like an intoxicant in the air. It's everywhere, but the pink are too high to realize it. The clown wants a big group of dead individuals, and one way to assure conformity is to standardize thought and expression.

Truth spliced with just a pinch of something else renders the whole thing 100% false.

The clown starts with a fundamental truth: *all people share equal access to the Father through Jesus.* Christ didn't die for some, he died for all. This is an absolute truth. But in order to hawk a crooked counterfeit concept, he had to splice this truth with something else. He had to make slight adjustments. Instead of saying that all of humanity has equal access to the Father through Jesus, the clown sold us on the notion that all of us are in fact *created equal* – thank you Thomas Jefferson and the Declaration of Independence. This is fundamentally not true, but the clown gets away with selling the counterfeit Rolex because most of us are ignorant and insecure. To say that everyone is created equal panders to our insecurity, but in actuality we are not created equal, we are created *unique*.

Put another way, if we were all created equal we'd share in spiritual uniformity by trait, and there would be no option to exercise individualism by choice. If we were all created equal, we'd all be named equally for our ambassadorship in the kingdom. If we were all created equal - to the clown's great satisfaction - God becomes a predator with a desire not for individual intimacy, but some sort of a stiff and unemotional group orgy. Understanding your unique individualism before Christ is step one on a multi-step process of fully appreciating your true kingdom identity. That's why this message is so corrosive and debilitating.

Pink Christian pacifists can't help but yearn for equality and fairness. Because it's a political buzzword with idealistic connotations, they ignorantly assume that *fairness* must be important to God as well. It's not. Justice is important to God. Fairness doesn't exist, couldn't exist, and by its very definition bucks against His desire for individual intimacy.

Some pink believers are adamant that equally cherished by God (Galatians 3, Romans 2, John 13) translates to equally gifted, equally created, equally engaged, and equally called to service on earth. Not so. If that was the case, you would not have heard stories about Samuel, David, Mary, Paul, Abraham, Esther or Job, just to name a few. These men and women were uniquely distinguished in the Word of God for a very unique set of circumstances, giftings, and expectations from the

Pink

Father.

Facebook now has something like 30 different categories of sexual orientation. The inclusive message in pop-culture seeks to generalize everyone and everything under one banner. Whether you sexually identify as a traditionalist or whether you identify as the love interest of the Amazonian Orc Spider - nobody is unique, and everyone must identify uniformly lest someone *feel* discriminated upon.

The US public school system, in the name of fairness, violently thrusts this same message at every opportunity. Unisex bathrooms, unisex locker rooms, unisex sports; it's all going to unisex everything. Then there is unisex in advertising, perfumes, clothing, and art. The message is everywhere. Equality, uniformity, fairness, inclusiveness, togetherness, mutual tolerance, the list goes on and on. These concepts sound great but are figments of our imagination. None of them actually exist in the kingdom of heaven, and most are pipedreams here on earth as well.

Life in the kingdom is not predicated on a horizontal identification, or valuation, of self-worth. Put another way, my individual experience with Christ is not better or worse than anybody else's. But all too often, the pink church relays uniformity messaging because the people are sensitive and unsure about who they are before God. They have no foundation of identity – *value* – based in their vertical relationship with Christ. Because of this lack of vertical identity, things like equality, uniformity, fairness and togetherness become very important as the pink stake their whole sense of spiritual value on them.

The kingdom result of the *You're Not Special* message stifles individualism while promoting a climate of division. This is because the message is primarily interested in defining acceptable degrees of thought and behavior, and in doing so, divisions erupt because not everyone is the same. Most of us have an ingrained bent toward individualism. *Correction:* **all of us** *have an ingrained bent toward individualism!*

At some level, the average Christian hates to be told what he/she can and cannot do in the context of relating to Christ Jesus or the kingdom as a whole. Division plays out in a typical cycle where the pink church splits in two, and one group with one set of ideals goes left while the other goes right. Each group doubles down on a litany of standards and the cycle repeats itself.

Say Peter musters the courage to defy his group's preset

boundaries of spiritual individualism. Let us also assume that he lacks a sense of vertical identity in Christ. The net result of this combination is oftentimes division and conflict. His group becomes agitated because he's doing things that don't jive with their status quo. Feeling newly ostracized, Peter's sense of value is rattled by his newfound lack of group identity. Maybe he starts looking for a crowd more aligned to his way of thinking, or maybe he decides to build one. Let's pretend he does the latter. Relying on his natural charisma and individual passion, he cultivates a new group commensurate with his idealistic standards of behavior. If he's successful, *poof,* the new-first-church-of-the-whatever is born on the corner of Get A Clue and Asinine Street, and the pink church marches forward.

Counterfeit messaging is everywhere in the pink church. The *You're Not Special* message is just one of many. Personally, I do not believe that most Christian leaders are willful deceivers. I think they're just people who struggle to understand their identity in Christ and lack clarity of calling. As such, it's impossible to lay the problems associated with counterfeit messaging exclusively at their feet.

If my engagement with Christ is directly predicated on my pastor's skill as an orator or the passion exhibited by the worship leader, then I am a big part of the problem. Christ didn't come to establish a refugee camp on the plains so we could live in spiritual obscurity while our pastor burns with passion on the mountain engulfed in flames. Sure, my pastor may not be adequately encouraging me to join him in the mountain… But ultimately, Christ is going to view my proximity to Him as a function of *my* responsibility, not my pastor's.

A couple years ago I had a vision in the middle of the day. In it, I found myself in a large house packed to the brim with people. There were two types of people inside. One group was injured, for lack of better descriptor. They had flesh wounds. They struggled with psychological disability. They were homeless, scared, and appeared to need help. The other group was feverishly trying to address the needs of the needy. Some were bandaging wounds, others were praying, or counseling, or whatever. At first glance, this appeared to be a picture of the kingdom at work in the lives of the lost.

Then I heard a loud *boom* coming from outside, and what had been a bright sunny day turned eerily orange. The lights in the house were not on, so the entire atmosphere dimmed inside the home as the atmosphere changed outside. The noise became louder so I advanced through the crowd and made it to the front door. Scared, I cracked it open and looked outside. There, descending on a bright fiery cloud was the throne of God and I heard a voice yell, "turn, and face the Lord!"

I ran inside the house and called upon the people to stop what they were doing and accompany me to the front yard so that we could face the Lord. I expected them to follow but they didn't. Pausing, I reasserted the message that I was getting from the Lord and called upon them to stop whatever they were doing and join me in the yard, but nobody stopped. It was as though they did not hear me. Fearing for their lives I started screaming for them to join me, but they would not stop what they were doing.

This vision was a clear picture of group-think. Collective, communal behavior. Sheep-people doing the stuff that they believe elevates their worth in the eyes of God, never realizing that worth was established not by their good deeds but by the love of the creator.

Many of us are actively engaged in various outreach ministries. We support missionaries, host home groups, give to charity and immerse ourselves in the communal activities of the local church. These activities are not bad - indeed, they are good and worthy endeavors - but if these works are being done at the expense of our ability to turn and face the Lord, the consequences will be dreadful. Why work if not for the glory of God? Why slave to the church's mission if it comes at the expense of our intimacy with the Father?

His concern is first and foremost for us as individuals. After that, He's interested in the collective efforts of the group as a whole, but never as a substitute for individual intimacy. *You* are more unique and special than you know. The gifts and graces that the Father has bestowed upon you are required - desperately needed - in the kingdom today. Your healthy engagement of the world around you, predicated on a vertical valuation of worth, deals a terrible blow to the efforts of the clown.

It's wrong to get caught up in groupthink but it sure is easy, isn't it? We *feel* a false sense of security in groupthink. Groupthink relinquishes us of our responsibility of self-determination; it's easy to follow the crowd. We are so used to being herded from one place to the next, that the idea of stepping out and pursuing a relationship of individuality with God through Christ is scary.

But the fact remains that I am the only person alive today - the only person in the history of our civilization - that has the ability to bring my unique expression of love to God. Nobody else can ever be a substitute for me, just as sure as I could never be a substitute for you. If you choose to engage Him as one of a million identical looking sheep-people, you will never fully realize what it is like to be loved by One who has a voracious capacity, and God will never know what it's like to be loved fully by you either.

You are special, and don't ever forget that.

Chapter 7 – Submission

Hebrews 13:17 says, *Obey your leaders and submit to them, for they keep watch over your souls as those who will give an account. Let them do this with joy and not with grief, for this would be unprofitable for you.*

Submission is confounding, isn't it? In theory, it shouldn't be difficult to submit to those we trust. Receiving counsel shouldn't be such a scary thing. Ideally, we all ought to be free givers and receivers of feedback to the betterment of our lives, but something always seems to hijack our good intentions, doesn't it? More often than not feedback serves to drive the wedge of division between us. Emotional wounds and hurts abound. My life experience counsels me against submitting to anyone. Life is easier without it. People have a tendency to make mistakes, furnish guidance based out of emotion and judge harshly.

The truth is submission was never meant to be what we've created it to be. Like masculine courage or feminine sagacity, submission is a powerful spiritual tool. Submission defies human understanding because it can only exist in the spirit realm where its essence is representative of a truth-principal. Submission is fundamentally important to the relational structures of the kingdom of heaven, and that is why the clown has gone to such great lengths to corrupt it in the minds of the pink. Let me explain.

True submission only manifests out of an identity rooted in the *vertical* paradigm. If I look at submission as an interaction between me and another human, I've missed the mark. I've fallen into the clown's trap. However, if I look at submission as an interaction between me and Christ, I've nailed it.

I do not submit to people and/or situations. I submit to Christ *in* people and/or situations. Christ asked me to live my life in the context of the authority structures He's created around me, so I choose to do just that. In this way I don't put my trust in the counsel or judgments of men and women; rather, I place my trust in Christ. Because my trust is in Christ and not the infallibility of another person, it becomes easier to navigate conflicts and potentially thorny relational dynamics associated with a submissive relationship.

Years ago, I rocketed up the chain of command and became a supervisor at a midsized company. I was zealous, energetic, and had some natural leadership gifting that helped move me along. Once I reached a supervisory role, I thrived for over a year and was extremely effective. But as time passed, I became a little too big for my britches and began treading outside of my role designation. I started doing my boss's job because I felt he was not being effective. The people I worked for were pretty immature, so rather than sit me down and address the concerns they had I was suddenly demoted and given the option to resign.

That experience challenged me to my core. I had derived a lot of *bad identity* from my leadership position, and to have it all ripped away was difficult. It rubbed coarsely against my pride. Because the demotion was so abrupt, I had no real option but to accept it and continue working for the company. I wanted nothing more than to quit and be done with that place, but over the course of a few weeks I was convicted about my lack of submission.

The Lord asked me why I was refusing to submit. My response was, "God, they don't deserve me! Why on earth should I submit to them?"

Though I was resistant at first, I began to understand that submission was never intended to be a gift that I choose whether or not to bestow on the authority around me. Like money, it was not mine to give or withhold from anyone. Submission is the relational currency of heaven. Whether I liked it or not and whether I understood it or not, the Lord made it clear that I was being required to submit to the exact men that had humiliated me, and there was nothing I could do about it.

Instead of quitting my job, I decided to spend the next few months working as hard as I could to magnify the bosses I despised. Not wanting my sacrifice to be in vain, I forced myself to stop despising them as well. That summer, as a result of my acquiescence to the power of submission, I actually came to appreciate them for the leaders that they were.

I didn't choose to submit and work my ass off because I felt like my bosses deserved me. I chose to work my ass off because I knew it was what God required. This was one of those lessons of humility along the pathway through the mountain ablaze. I volunteered to work the toughest shifts and with the toughest youth.

Through this experience, I realized that submission was not about doing something for someone else, nor was it about doing something because an authority figure tells me to. Submission was simply a function of my life, required by the

Lord. Though the experience of coming to realize this truth was difficult on my pride, His goodness came full-circle and I was better off having submitted than I would've been had I quit in anger.

The pink church (in unity with the hurting lost) categorizes submission as the act of becoming someone else's doormat, stepstool, or whipping post. That's not what submission is, that's what abuse is. Submission is not something that a leader can require of a subordinate, it's not something that a husband can require of his wife, and it's not something that a boss can require of an employee. True submission can only come by way of a volunteer offering. The submitted must offer it freely. The husband must offer it freely. The wife must offer it freely. The children must offer it freely. The employee must offer it freely. Friends must offer it freely to one another.

In a marriage, wives are required to submit to their husbands by firm commandment in Scripture (Ephesians 5:22, Colossians 3:18), but they often choose not to for fear of abuse. Others choose not to out of ignorance of what submission actually is. Scripture doesn't call upon wives to submit to husbands because the husband deserves it. Submission manifests in our physical relationships but it's an act of intimacy toward the Father in heaven *first*.

What exactly does this mean? Simply, it means that if a disagreement arises in the home, submission (as a spiritual tool) is there to assure that the matter doesn't turn into a full-fledged knockout fight between husband and wife. Submission does not mean that the couple must make big decisions right away. Submission allows both, husband and wife, to bury the emotional hatchet and let cooler heads prevail. If used, it is a wildly sagacious method to conflict resolution when the clown is attempting to drive a wedge between you and your loved one. But submission is not merely a component of the marriage relationship. It's everywhere.

Within the church, we the people are required to submit to the eldership by firm commandment in Scripture (Hebrews 13:17), but we often choose not to out of fear. Who wants to be transparent and open before a "holy man"? Scripture also commands that we submit one to another out of our reverence for Christ (Ephesians 5:21). Uniformly it's clear that the submission is the relational currency of heaven, so a right understanding of it is of paramount importance.

At times when I've withheld submission, I've experienced a loss of peace in my life. Similarly, I stagnate from a revelatory standpoint as well. This is because a lack of submission correlates to misplaced trust. Misplaced trust correlates to a lack of intimacy with Christ. A lack of intimacy with Christ correlates to a lack of peace and limited revelation.

Here in Colorado, marijuana was recently approved for recreational consumption. As a result, Christian men and women who liked the idea of their newfound freedom, predictably, have had issues with elders that counsel on the basis of kingdom-based lifestyles. If authentic submission exists, the gonj-smoker should be able to receive the wisdom of his/her eldership as *good counsel* and nothing more. The person ought to be able to chew up the meat and spit out the bones according to his or her own individual relationship with Christ Jesus. Being able to receive feedback and apply it to individualized decision-making is in effect, submission.

Unfortunately, true submission is in short supply along the streets of tent-city. Typically, the person submitting ends up despising good counsel on the basis of its implied judgment of wrongdoing. Anyone who lacks the ability to submit lacks true identity in Christ. If the submitter enjoyed identity firmly rooted in Christ, he likely understands that good counsel is different from judgment… It's just good counsel.

Good leaders will bring counsel and correction to young believers. That's their job. But if young believers lack submission, they end up getting frustrated and eventually rebel. In rebellion, submissive engagement with the church is untenable. And without submission, there can be no growth of intimacy in Christ. This is why submission is so important.

Voluntary submission places the burden of accountability on the leader, or the one who has been given the authority to govern. In a marriage, when a woman voluntarily submits to her husband she is simultaneously relinquishing responsibility for wrongdoing, as is her right under God. Thereby, the responsibility of governance becomes a burden that the husband must carry, and failure to lead his family with integrity and pure motivation will eventually come around to bite him.

In the church, when the congregation submits to the leadership, the elders are the ones who inherit the responsibilities of governance, and they are the ones who are credited with its success or failure. This is why it is written, "To him who is given much, much is expected." (Luke 12:48) If elders fail to lead with integrity, theirs is inevitably going to be a long and painful fall. In the judgment that befalls them, the people are spared because they did what was right in the eyes of God by submitting.

The Lord never wanted leaders to exercise bad authority over the rest of us, and knows there is a tendency toward corruption in this fallen world. He does not tell the weak to submit to the powerful so that the powerful have an all-encompassing ability to exercise their abusive and dictatorial authority. He implores people to submit to authority so that when He judges the wickedness of bad leaders, the people can be spared. He calls us to submit one to another so that if anyone is ever caught outside the submitted body of Christ, that person is easily identified as a stranger. Submission is not something required of women and minorities alone. Submission is required living for every believer, the world over.

Submission is a tool of righteousness, not an act of weakness. It's time the pink church realized how effective this tool is against the clown's menacing attacks. We use a comparative pocket knife called *guilt* and *shame* to ward off the clown's onslaught when we ought to be experimenting with the bazooka of spiritual warfare known as *submission*. Is the pink church really going to swallow Madonna's best interpretation of a concept that's way beyond her, and subsequently claim wisdom? Please...

You don't need to sit at anyone's feet and hope for

crumbs or warm milk - and I don't care whether we are talking about a bad husband or bad church leadership. Yours is first and foremost a vertical relationship directly with Christ, so keep your focus vertical. But as we submit one to another on a horizontal plane, we exercise our right to live righteously in the image of Christ, and this comes with a profound reward. We are given spiritual protections, and we inherit a special grace that softens the coarseness of life's day-to-day challenges. We find nourishment when we live righteously. We find energy when we live righteously. We find strength and wisdom when we stop and make a conscientious decision to live righteously.

The wellspring of spiritual revelation comes through intimacy with Christ. Living in His kingdom according to His relational currency (submission) is a huge step toward intimacy. By submitting, you're telling the universe that the abuses commonplace on earth cannot and will not keep you from the one you love. By submitting, you push back against the clown when he tries to rob you of the joys of relationship. By submitting, you claim intimacy with Christ through action and deed and His reciprocal advance toward you is earth shattering!

Submission can only be wielded by a courageous and sagacious person. If you simply can't submit to the authorities that God has established around you, then you are neither courageous nor sagacious and likely have a pink complexion. And, to the super naïve: no, disagreement is not abuse. You don't get to stop living in submission because the authority structure in your life doesn't share your view on things.

God never gave kingdom leaders the right to consolidate power and authority. Forced consolidation of authority only comes by way of evil men in the fallen Earth. Even the Son of God, Jesus, spent his ministry earning his leadership position through the voluntary submission of the disciples and those around him. The only way leaders will begin walking out their unique leadership design is when people around them voluntarily submit. Think about this in the context of your husband or church leader. If you are still living in your parents' house, think about this in the context of your relationship to them. They can't become great leaders to *you* if you never let them. If you refuse to submit, you withhold their ability to lead.

Do you see the connotation here? The one who submits actually has the power, not the other way around. In the kingdom of heaven, leaders cannot compel followers through force. It's not the way God made His kingdom. But when we approach this kingdom with human eyes, we run the risk of misunderstanding all sorts of important variations. His is a spiritual kingdom, one that is built on the principles of absolute truth. We cannot abide in that kingdom with fallen eyes and an earthly perspective. To fully abide in the kingdom of God is to accept the principles on which that kingdom was founded, much like we choose to accept the laws of nature on earth.

I submit to Christ vertically, and he requires that I submit to the authority structure around me. I willingly accept this requirement not just because the principle is sound, but because I've been doing it long enough to know that it is truly good for me.

Chapter 8 – The Horizontal Hierarchy

The *horizontal hierarchy* is what I call the manmade structures of governance within the religious entity. The horizontal hierarchy is a top-down system of governance that is controlled by the established leaders within the pink church. Because people control it (horizontal) it's heavily concerned with who has the ultimate authority to settle disputes of Christian policy and procedure, as well as who has the authority to speak revelation and interpret Scripture. The horizontal hierarchy is a spiritual lineage passed down from the Pharisees and Sadducees of old.

Contrast that with *vertical hierarchy*. The vertical hierarchy is a system of governance that is established and maintained by God. The vertical hierarchy is not established or managed by man, and it's why freak-shows like John the Baptist, Elisha or Jesus could have ever been successful at what they set out to do. Had it been up to the managers of the horizontal hierarchy, these 'blasphemers' would've been burned at the stake. ...and oftentimes were, but not before God's purposes were fulfilled.

It is no secret that many of us have at one point or

another become upset with the church. I have a lot of friends who are on-again/off-again with respect to their local fellowship, and I know even more people who have literally said "to hell with it all," and left the classical *church* altogether. What is it about church that sparks such an outrage? You don't see people throwing up their hands, kicking the dirt, and emotionally acting out of their disappointment in the local Lions Club.

For me, disenchantment with the church came as a result of my own misplaced trust. It came as a result of my adherence to the horizontal hierarchy. Sure, an argument can be made that some church leaders bait people into unhealthy person-to-church relationships, but I'm convinced that misplaced trust is normally a product of immaturity and fear within the individual. At least it was in my case. It was I who adopted unhealthy expectations of the church, in other words, not the other way around.

Some time ago I was talking to a friend of mine, who although doesn't attend a classical *church* regularly, is viewed as a spiritual father-figure nevertheless. He's jam-packed with wisdom, leads his family with dignity and courage, and is good with his money. He has been given the so-called "right hand of fellowship" from established Christian leaders, and has been commissioned by that leadership structure to pastor those in his circle, although outside of the traditional arrangement. This friend of mine has, on many occasions, told me that he submits to an established leadership core, and identifies those individuals within that core by name. Now, this friend and I have a transparent association and years of friendship to our credit, so I can get away with making critical observations. There is no unhealthy wielding of authority between us.

With the relational credit that I possessed, I challenged his leadership position by making the observation, "I'm having a hard time seeing the difference between your leadership in this hybrid structure and the horizontal hierarchy commonplace within the failing church." This comment, predictably, led to an interesting discussion.

The people, *His* people, have always gravitated toward tent-city, located a sufficient distance away from the mountain ablaze with the majesty of God's manifest presence. Tent-city is located in an IDP camp (Internally Displaced People). Different from a refugee camp, an IDP camp is established when displaced and homeless people find shelter together in the midst of political unrest inside the boundaries of their home country. I like this visual because tent-city located inside an IDP camp is firmly inside the home country of Christianity.

Pink

As I note in the prologue to this book, it is populated by Christians firmly established in their country of origin, but homeless and poverty stricken by virtue of their graven images and rejection of the living God. It's not as though the pink church is living in a refugee camp, outside the home country of Christianity, for we all share in the idealistic hope of where we're headed - the promised land.

The pink church and the industry of Christianity has become the central marketplace of the IDP camp. I'll come back to this visual a lot throughout the rest of this book.

Think back to Moses and the Israelites. Then, like now, the people preferred to distance themselves from things that frightened them. By keeping a healthy distance from God, we the people get to live without ever having to make sense of God's values, many of which seem counterintuitive to the human experience. By living at a distance, we retain a sense of ownership and self-determination that we assume would otherwise evaporate in close proximity to the mountain. But because the crisis of life confounds our best efforts of navigation, we send an emissary, an information liaison out to the mountain to decipher the will of the Almighty, and thereby hope to ingratiate ourselves to Him. Enter Moses - or feel free to splice in any other name of any other leader you'd like.

We tell Moses to go and decipher the codes and report back. We presumptuously tell our new leader to do and say whatever he must to keep God from becoming angry. We tell him to intercede on our behalf, and charge him with the responsibility of keeping the God-man relationship fresh. We tell him that he speaks for the group, and commend ourselves for the brilliance behind the idea of one voice for one God.

At the behest of the people, the Moses-like leader goes and does just that. But he soon realizes something unexpected. He realizes that God is not an enigma or riddle at all. He comes to understand that God is shockingly simplistic in His expectations of us, and remarkably intimate in His desire for relationship. Excited, the leader comes back and tries to spread the good news!

"No, no… It's not like that. God actually likes us. He actually wants to be with us, and he really wants to meet you, too."

The leader hears crickets. Nobody speaks. This leader's proclamation makes no sense to the people living in the IDP camp. The message of kindness and gentleness grates against a worldview that's been ingrained by the whispers of a sycophantic clown. Our experience in life has taught us to believe that nothing comes without a price, and that there is no such thing as a free lunch.

When a lie feels so much like truth, it's not easily abandoned.

Fast-forward.

In the first century A.D. the modern church sprang to life out of the seeds that were sown by the Apostles. On the testimony of eyewitness accounts, people heard and many believed in the message of the gospel. Fundamentally, the message of the gospel was that Christ came, died, and rose again for the purpose of an eternal love affair. It was an *intimate* sacrifice, performed for the one-on-one relationships that He so desired would sprout and blossom throughout the generations.

He didn't die so that the church would spring to life and impart wisdom and hierarchy to the individual; he died so that the individual would spring to life and grow into maturity. In banding with others who chose to do the same, they'd behave out of the unique graces of gift mixes they possessed in Christ and become the *Church*.

Some of us understood this so we knocked on doors, searched the dark alleys, and courageously dove deep into our own hearts in a radical pursuit to find the One who first loved us. Tent-city was not enough. Some of us sprinted to the mountain ablaze and risked having the skin melt off our bones in the heat, deciding that it was worth it to know Him in truth. To pursue the Father through a mountain ablaze requires courage and fortitude, the type of courage and fortitude not common on earth. Indeed, this type of courage only comes through trust well-placed in the goodness of God.

In this way I pursued, and I did so with absolute conviction. The pursuit was hard at times. If you've never traversed the steep cliffs of fear and doubt, take it from somebody who knows... It can get really tough. But eventually, out of the gloom of self-hatred and rebellion, Christ came and extended a perfectly clean hand to the decaying one attached my wrist. Confused, disoriented, and gasping for air I reached up. As I touched his outstretched fingers, a radical power flashed forth and entered me, like a bolt of lightning. In that power I found the wisdom to speak truth and the courage to defy mortal fear. The same defiance that gave Christ the grace to be slaughtered is freely given to you and me through the Spirit of power.

One effect of experiencing that power encounter with the Lord is that we are emboldened, almost instantaneously. Upon returning to the IDP camp, the budding leader stands and begins to speak truth as perceived through a new experience with a wondrous and infinite God. Those who lack the courage to pursue for themselves clamor about, and ask leading questions about what it's like in the kingdom of heaven.

"Tell me about His love… Does He really see me that way?"

"Do I have to give up masturbation…?"

"So say I believe you… What's the catch?"

"If I follow you there, will I still be allowed to drink and go out with my friends?"

"… Will I have to go to church?"

"No!" The young leader says, ramming his fist into his opened palm. "You don't get it, the whole entire paradigm shifts. Questions you think are worthy on this temporal earth would never get so much as a neurological backfire in the eternal kingdom of heaven. What was counterintuitive, gawky, and seemed ill-conceived as a blind half-wit is illuminated in truth when, with courage and sagacity, you make personal choices to reject the lies of the clown and pursue the heart of God."

That young leader, having realized truth in Christ, then becomes intertwined in a web of chaos in tent-city. People who adamantly refuse to part ways with the clown's lies force the leader into the emissary role once again. Like Moses, the one who pursued and found truth becomes the next in a long line of information liaisons, *and the pink goo flows through the IDP camp, cascading from the doors of the church...* And the church bleeds, and the people are rocked with confusion, and our beloved Savior is ever misunderstood. Why? For what?

Just enough is understood to begin establishing a much-needed order and hierarchy within the IDP camp. This then leads to the birth of the horizontal hierarchy. Leaders are promoted on the basis of their ability to assure order, not on the basis of their experience with the Father. Maintaining order is of paramount importance because a mob in the IDP camp could destroy it.

... Like a beast trying to tear the pink sheep off those

Pink

hooks…

New leaders are promoted on the basis of their charisma, magnetism, and ability to not ever offend the minds of the feeble. True emissaries traverse the expanse between IDP camp and mountain ablaze, but the marketplace gets rich and the people die because a message birthed in truth is stifled, said to be offensive, and blotted out as heresy.

In order for the pink church to heal, what needs to change is not doing away with the brick and mortar. The gathering place is awesome. Why are we taking our frustrations out on the gathering place? What needs to change is the message. Those of us who have encountered the mountain do Him a great disservice if we accept the commission appointed by the people to be a representative voice on *their* behalf. Christ doesn't want to hear from Tom, Dick, or Harry through me. He never did. He wants to know Tom, Dick, and Harry individually.

So preoccupation with titles, things like Pastor, Elder, Apostle or Deacon is modern Sadducee-ism, plain and simple, and it's an abomination.

One might ask: why do well-meaning, radical pursuers of

Christ's heart find themselves ensnared in this trap? How come the leaders accept the information liaison appointment and pull back from doing everything they can to deliver the absolute truth behind Christ's desires for an eternal love affair? How come they get so hung up on the roles and responsibilities of elders, pastors, teachers, equippers, small group hosts, potluck organizers, children's teachers and the like? What's with their incessant need to define who somebody is relative to their horizontal structures of hierarchy?

In a privileged room and among themselves they say, "Well, Jared has a keen gift in the prophetic…"

"Yes, true, but I see an emerging grace for evangelism…"

Why do leaders fall victim to this trickery? Because the clown is a centuries-old master of the dark arts and we have an awful tendency to misplace our trust. That's why.

Some leaders get snared in the clown's trap pertaining to doctrine. They can't help but worry about the authenticity of their doctrine, and what is a healthy exercise becomes an unhealthy obsession. If the leader were to step out of the way and give his flock - or neighbors, or whoever's within his/her sphere of authority - a swift kick in the ass while telling them,

"The truth is, I don't really know if it's right for you to quit your job. There's the burning mountain right up ahead. Go find out for yourself!" then he runs the risk of losing some control over the message.

The clown's playbook has never changed. 2000 years ago he convinced the Pharisees that doctrine was far and away more important to God than the hearts and lives of people. Same-old, same-old today, but I ask you this… If the clown is as effective at corrupting simple truth as Bill Belichick is at bringing home AFC championships, why re-create the wheel?

Other leaders can't help but worry about the tithe and attendance of their gatherings. What was once a radical pursuit of passion has become a job because the clown has piggybacked on a truthful message about their call and purpose to the generation, and corrupted that message by splicing in the responsibility of provision. When a leader convinces himself that provision is a function of his own responsibility, the rest is a long and dark falling away from intimacy. He's out of the game. The anointing bestowed upon him by the Lord remains in effect, but his effectiveness has been dramatically compromised, his reward in heaven has been plundered, and the people who are duped by his greed and lack of faith sometimes suffer awful consequences.

Some of these so-called leaders in the pink church have become so brazen and hardened that if you get them a little tipsy, they start singing to the high heavens about what an amazing gig they fell into! "Yeah brother, shepherding a flock is what I was made to do! Heck, the pay ain't so bad either…"

This hardened and destructive agent of the clown will tell you it was a blessing; he'll even swear that his life is a testimony about how God will make your life easier if you just trust. The truth is, at the expense of his Lord's kingdom, this crooked General has decided to become a bribe taker, a swindler, a money launder. There are more of these shysters running around the IDP camp then you could possibly imagine. This is why in Matthew 7:22-23 Jesus asserts, "In that day many will come and say to me Lord, Lord I did all these things in your name. But I will say to them, 'depart from me you evildoer, for I never knew you'."

Crooked shysters, they are a dime a dozen, running around the IDP camp in comparative luxury and feigning a sense of wisdom and piety. These guys will never curse, and you'll never see them malign another's character. This is because they are masterful at promoting the lie. But I am convinced that short of repentance, these men and women will be consigned to the pit of hell in the end. They are wolves in sheep's clothing and have figured out how to make the kingdom of God their personal hedge fund.

You might be thinking, "That seems a bit harsh, Nate…"

Is it? There are so many of these people leading the church today that the entire kingdom has been hoisted up on rusty meat hooks, and become the plaything of a sadomasochistic clown. We need to open our eyes.

The horizontal hierarchy came about because when leaders return from the mountain with unexpected information about the loving nature of God, the people refused to become His kingdom. When leaders tell us that the deity wants to be *their* individual God, and that He wanted them to be His individual people, they were obliged to say no.

It might have gone something like this.

"Thanks, but no thanks," the tent dwellers say. "We prefer to live here in tent-city. And Moses, while you're at it, tell that dude we prefer to have a King as well. See if He'd be cool with an arrangement that's a little more tangible and user-friendly on our end…"

"That's what they said?" The Lord thought about it for a minute. He knows that would never work, he knows that a horizontal hierarchy would bring about a ton of pain and suffering, not the least of which would be the pain and suffering He'd have to put His own Son through. …But alas, God so loved the world that he would indeed send his one and only Son…

"Fine, they can have it their way. I suppose this is the price that I must pay for an everlasting love affair with volunteer hearts."

"It seems like a steep price," Moses replies.

"Oh but it's not," God responds, "I assure you, there is nothing like the volunteer heart of the lover…"

The horizontal was not concocted by evil and malicious man in this generation. This thing is as ancient as life on earth. I criticize the horizontal hierarchy because it was never supposed to be this way, for any of us. We were never supposed to be subject to the bondage that the horizontal effectuates. It's not man's responsibility to build the kingdom; it's our responsibility to live by truth and spread the good news of salvation through grace. By choosing to abide individually, the kingdom naturally populates. But sadly, there will always be a Christian *industry* because there will always be cowards who refuse to lay hold of their own relationship responsibilities and live by a kingdom identity.

This is a relevant message for this generation because the era of the horizontal hierarchy is drawing to an end, so to speak. It will never be abolished, but it will disseminate relative to the expansion of the vertical hierarchy in the years to come. A great harvest is approaching. The IDP camp is ill-equipped to deal with a resurgence of kingdom truth, but truth is coming by the new wines of revelation whether the tent dwellers like it or not.

Chapter 9 – The Vertical Hierarchy

Vertical hierarchy cannot exist unless we dispense with our ingrained religious sensitivities. Religiosity - unhealthy addiction to the laws that govern individual expressions of intimacy - is like acid to metal. It corrodes our ability to experience Him in truth. This is why the spirit of religion is such a powerful current within the pink church. The clown uses it to stifle individual expression.

Dispensing with religiosity has the potential to offend the naturally sensitive, and that's why this chapter may confront the reader in unique ways. Though dispensing with sensitivities may be uncomfortable, it is wholly necessary if we are to ever experience Christ authentically.

The vertical hierarchy is based in one simple truth: Christian unity begins with agreement about the Trinitarian Godhead, and ends with agreement about the divinity of Christ Jesus, and that's it.

Unity can never befall a group of people who have 50,000 different opinions about 50,000 different nuances of doctrinal absolutes. In my youth, I was the type of person who derived spiritual value on my ability to debate nuance. By winning a debate - at least as far as I could tell - I felt a rush of justification. My justification led to a counterfeit sense of righteousness. Debate is a horizontal pursuit.

There is a huge difference between a young inquisitive mind and a spirit that demands to be valued on the basis of how correct it is. It wasn't until I began valuing myself on the basis of the vertical hierarchy structure that I overcame the corrosion of religiosity.

When Jesus toured around with his disciples, I missed where he interrogated Mary Magdalene about her sexual history. I missed where He went around and asked, before sitting down to eat in a stranger's home, whether or not the host was gay. I can't remember a single instance where He asked the disciples how they swung politically. Can you?

Those were the kind of questions that the Pharisees asked, not Jesus. When the disciples puffed up their chest over who was to be more revered in the kingdom to come, did He not dismiss them as petulant children? He dismissed them because they were seeking value based in religiosity.

Preoccupation with endless questions about law permeates the horizontal hierarchy because systems and structures and rules are what keep the horizontal power structure in place. In the horizontal, a person's ideology is of great importance because noncompliance represents a significant and imminent threat to the clown's vice grip on the people.

What then did Jesus actually ask? What was the extent of His kingdom's politics?

"Who do they say that I am?"

If we are to experience Him in truth, this is the only close-fisted question that has any eternal relevance. All other subsequent mysteries of the faith are revealed through simple conviction about the Trinitarian Godhead and the divinity of Christ Jesus.

The vertical hierarchy can only exist if the people volunteer to sprint with radical, courageous abandonment straight into the heart of the burning mountain. But it's impossible to enter if tied down by religiosity. Religiosity must be checked at the door. The sensitivities that come by way of a religious spirit must also be checked at the door. In the mountain, those things go from being seemingly good lifestyle boundaries, to erected barriers between we the people and Christ.

This is because inside the mountain, revelation is not imparted by the nuances of doctrine but by the power of God's changing work on our lives. The clown will still tempt and we will still struggle to define truth along the path of healing, but revelation comes by a power that far transcends the authority of rules.

In the vertical hierarchy structure, the leader points the way to the mountain, but it's the people who assume responsibility for their individual love affairs. In the vertical hierarchy, leaders don't worry about promoting fellow leaders from within - as though they need a succession plan for when King David or the Prophet Samuel keel over and die - because such planning is irrelevant. This is because God has taken responsibility for the establishment of leaders, and will promote individuals according to His will and timing. Sometimes this establishment might include an ordination by way of some sort of ceremonial activity, but I don't see the scriptural basis for a bunch of pomp and circumstance. In the vertical hierarchy, leadership will naturally speak, prophesy, blog and write their way onto a predestined platform of authority according to His will and timing.

Some might ask, "How can this be? What if a false teacher rises up? If there is no authoritative vetting process, how can we know who to trust?"

Who's fretting about being duped? Do we not currently abide in the pink IDP camp of watered down teaching and religious absolute?

An interesting byproduct of grafting our identity to the mountain is that we inherit the ability to judge right from wrong, and truth from a lie. Mountain dwellers know the difference between somebody who is promoted by the enemy/man and somebody who is promoted by God because we learn how to identify good fruit in the lives of His chosen. That good fruit bears witness with the spirit of Christ living inside us. Mountain dwellers no longer live in a world that demands visual evidence, for they live in a world where truth endorses itself by the spirit.

Our right and responsibility to judge is supported scripturally in John 7:24, *stop judging by mere appearances, but instead judge correctly…*

Also in 1 Corinthians 6:2, *or do you not know that the Lord's people will judge the world? And if you are to judge the world, are you not competent to judge trivial cases?*

The promise of true discernment in Christ Jesus is supported in John 10:27, *my sheep listen to my voice; I know them, and they follow me.*

If the promise of accurate judgment in Christ is the cake, do we not retain the icing of healthy human endorsement? In the vertical hierarchy, we no longer rely exclusively on a leader's endorsement of another leader. Instead we rely primarily on individual revelation that comes through intimacy with Christ, and secondarily retain the perk of healthy human endorsement.

Even if we agree that the vertical hierarchy works in theory, the transition from horizontal to vertical can be a little uncomfortable. You may find that dispensing with religious sensitivities - the act of unhooking yourself from the clown's entanglement - is your greatest challenge. It was for me. What does dispensing with religious sensitivities look like? I find it easiest to articulate this next point by giving an example from my own life.

I am not qualified to write this book according to the horizontal hierarchy structure. No Christian leader ever gave me permission to speak on behalf of the kingdom in this manner. But according to the vertical hierarchy I am compelled to deliver this message nevertheless. As I act out of my conviction, you must embrace your responsibility to judge and choose whether the message is authentic.

I become less than feeble and lizard-like when I engage in group-identity and interact with Christ as a one in a collective. No courage is required if I am a nameless, faceless, voiceless member of a group. No sagacity is required when the group makes all my decisions for me. By being one of many, I literally forgo all responsibilities to the kingdom. I become one of one in the kingdom when I live according to the vertical, but I am only one of an innumerable sum if I forgo the vertical and rely on the horizontal.

Take this book as an example. Is my delivery of this message spot on? No. In the vertical hierarchy I must rely on the grace Christ gives the reader if I am to hope that the message will serve its intended purpose. Not so with the horizontal. If I were writing from a horizontal perspective, I must assume the responsibility of perfection so as not to offend someone's feeble little lizard brain. This is because in the horizontal, the receiver relies on the messenger's courage and sagacity while in the vertical, the messenger relies on yours. The vertical places the onus of kingdom responsibility on the individuals within the group, where the horizontal places the onus of responsibility on the leadership.

The vertical perspective is authentically true because the Lord has never asked us to water down a message to appease the lowest common denominator. Why? Because the lower third in any pink room is comprised of wolves and kingdom hijackers. Why on earth would I worry about appeasing Pharaoh's sensibility or Caiaphas's misplaced religious identity? When I water it down, I merely reinforce their entanglement while doing everybody else a terrible injustice.

The horizontal caters to the weakest among us, and makes no distinction between friend and foe. The vertical caters to Christ only, and assumes His goodness in all circumstance.

Christ tells me that our manifest destiny is to be co-heirs of the kingdom of God. And as such, we are unfit to be perpetually *fucked* by a sadistic clown.

Did that pinpoint accurate four-letter word offend you? It

offends me too. But what offends me more is that the clown is doing exactly *that* by robbing me of my inheritance in Christ. And so long as I'm on the topic, I'm even more offended by the fact that he's doing *that* to my precious little daughter, daily.

Assuming we've dispensed with our sensitivities, let us move on. In the land of vertical hierarchy there is but one rule. *Submit to Christ, and Christ alone.* That's it. What's interesting about this rule is that by choosing to submit to Christ and Christ alone, adherers naturally subject themselves to the authorities that Christ establishes around them. Sometimes it's Caesar, or it's the IRS, or maybe it's a Christian brother, or a secular sister. Sometimes it's a kid, and sometimes it's the fully fallible Pope (regardless of his assertions to the contrary). If we are being honest with one another, it may one day be the death squad. I choose to submit to the authority that Christ has set around me because I choose to submit to Him. It is my free will to do so, but as an ambassador of His kingdom I am also compelled.

Spiritually, I don't submit to any one pastor, preacher, or elder per se, but I do submit to them all at one level or another. Even the ones that I suspect are a little pink. The level to which I receive spiritual counsel from the authority around me depends heavily on my experience with that particular individual. It depends heavily on whether or not his/her words are jiving with my spirit. It depends heavily on whether or not his/her counsel is in line with my understanding of the heart of God. And yes, it also depends on whether or not those I trust endorse the person speaking to me. There are many factors that inform how urgently I receive counsel, but I will always hear them out.

Why? Because whether I'm being counseled in truth or tempted by a lie, my behavior is ultimately my responsibility. I no longer have to fret about whether or not someone is delivering truth, as though I'm an infant and can't discern truth for myself, because I know truth by virtue of my pursuit vertically.

Some authority figures will respond to this book and criticize me for aspects of my delivery. No doubt about it. When they do, regardless of who they are, I shall fully submit to their feedback and will retain the right, according to my adherence to the vertical hierarchy, to chew up the meat and spit out the bones.

When they tell me that I risk alienating a certain readership by using things like four letter words, they're right. They're absolutely right. I submit to their authority of judgment and agree with their evidence. Does that mean I'll choose not to use a four letter word? Maybe. Maybe not. It depends on the context of the message. It depends fully on what I feel the Lord wants me to convey.

Submission has to do with acknowledging the authority of those around us and honoring their wisdom, counsel, and point of view *as though it were always in pinpoint alignment with that of Christ's*. But they aren't always in alignment, and they certainly aren't Christ. They are human. As human, they may become ensnared in one of the clown's traps just as I, or anyone might. So rather than place the fallible human on a pedestal of infallibility, I acknowledge their propensity to discern truth and receive it as such, and then promptly dissect the message with Christ in the mountain.

If by submitting we abort the step of dissecting the message with Christ, and automatically do and say according to how the authority figure instructs, we run the risk of making the authority figure *infallible* in our lives. Some pink Christians are so insecure that they will do anything their authority figure tells them to in the interest of preserving a conflict-free relationship. How else do you figure a guy like Jim Jones was able to talk his minions into mass suicide? He was made to be infallible by the people.

Pink

Authority figures are sometimes just as sensitive and insecure as the pink sheep. They might become upset if, as an example, I hear their counsel about four letter words and decide to use them anyway. But if you are an authority figure, why get upset about that? If I use them in rebellion, no skin off your back because I'll eventually have to suffer the consequences of my misstep with Christ. If I use them in truth, no loss of reward for you because I'm still the one that's gonna be waged for making the right decision.

Some people wrongly believe that the spiritual war is an impersonal one. Not true. The clown is not about shooting you from a nearby rooftop with a high caliber gun. Oh no. The clown is about coming up behind you, stroking his hands along the sensitive parts of your body, whispering sweet nothings, and making you think he's a friend. Once it's sticky and personal, he wraps his thin fingers around your throat and gazes longingly into your eyes as he squeezes the life right out of you.

Sure, the clown is thrilled with your apathy but he wants more than that. He wants you to suffer. He wants you to despair. He wants to watch as you take in the sights and sounds of hell and become a hopeless mess.

True engagement of the vertical paradigm requires that we come to the mountain just as we are; naked, hungry, and fiercely passionate about our need for truth. As we choose to stop quarreling with one another about doctrinal nuances and firmly submit to Christ and Christ alone, there is no limit to what He can do in our lives. If you shake off the yolk of religiosity, He'll clothe you instead with white linen, put a ring on your finger, and announce a kingdom celebration. For everyone who enters the mountain from the IDP camp is in effect, the prodigal son come home.

Chapter 10 - New Eyes

It is impossible to fully comprehend certain truths when relying on human eyes. New eyes in the spirit are what illuminate a world governed by principalities, and inform us on how to survive. Spiritually speaking, there is no way to get from point A - where we become convinced in the truth of Christ to point Z - where we have walked into the fullness of our authority in Christ, without first negotiating the many points of spiritual growth in between.

New eyes don't just happen upon us; they are a thing that develops over time. And not just over time, but over time *well spent* in the mountain. New eyes do not open wide as we attempt to hop, skip, and jump over the many points of spiritual upbringing. All that does is cause us to have to start over again. It's a progressive steady cyclical upbringing in Christ that is foolproof. We cannot fake maturity in Him.

Years ago when I hit my "point A", I was mesmerized by the teachings I heard in church. Amazing wisdom seems to come from everywhere, and was regularly expressed by the believing community around me. I ate it all up. I was always hungry for more, and in the beginning there were a lot of wellsprings to drink from.

Over time however, I found that I was getting less and less of the nourishment I wanted from the people around me, and more from Scripture and my time alone with God. It was as though the wellspring of spiritual revelation sort of dried up among the people, and if I wanted to glean nuggets of new revelation I could only get those from direct sources.

It wasn't too big of a deal in the beginning because I still had places to nourish myself, and I eagerly pursued those. But in time, something strange happened. I came to a place in my own walk that suddenly felt isolative and awkward. Though I lived among many, I felt we had somehow become disjointed, no longer unified in our experience or expressions of faith. I found it difficult to buy into some of the stuff I was seeing and hearing in the church. Naturally, I stepped away from heavy spiritual engagement and fell more easily into routines with nonbelievers. Likely, many of you have experienced something similar.

Simply put, my spirit was offended by the hypocrisy. I wasn't offended by people's lifestyle or their lifestyle counsel. Rather, my struggle had to do with a conflict that was much deeper and more elusive than that. It had to do with relational pretension. It had to do with denominational warfare; this need for everyone to try and compete for the right of absoluteness. It had to do with a spiritual undercurrent of greed, competition and compromise. Worst of all was a pervasive denial about the existence of these corrosive agents within the pink sheep at large.

I wrestled with this conflict for years. On one side I felt pretty strongly that some of what was being said by the men and women I respected was flat-out untrue. I struggled with their refusal to identify spiritual principalities that had clearly overtaken the encampment. On the other side, in my immaturity I felt that if I voiced concern or tried to confront the discrepancies, I was somehow backsliding or failing to live subject to the God-ordained structure of His kingdom on earth. In hindsight I now know that by my own immaturity, I had placed certain individuals on an unhealthy pedestal in my life and according to those misgivings did not think that I could buck their counsel.

It was a form of idolatry on my part. On one side God was showing me things through new eyes, and on the other side I denied those truths on the basis of the infallibility I prescribed to the men and women I trusted. They didn't tell me they were infallible, quite the contrary. I put them on that pedestal and by doing so I became neutered and cut away from participating in the greater discussions.

In all honesty I am not far removed from these exact hang-ups. For me, the man-pleasing spirit has been a real challenge for the bulk of my adult life, and it rears its ugly head even now from time to time.

It's been my experience that new eyes come as a result of time in the mountain. They are the manifestation of a trust bond between Christ and His beloved. As you traverse the peaks and valleys of your own journey into the mountain, the Lord will endow you with increasing measures of wisdom (sagacity) relative to the courage you display by trudging onward.

New eyes are not only valuable in identifying hypocrisy; they also inform us about the emotional side of God. They are a credit to our growth in Him. New eyes enable us to define kingdom values, which enable us to establish firm foundations for life in this decaying world. New eyes illuminate the mysteries that confound the wise, and enable the grace to find understanding and assurance in those things that have been hidden from the lost.

The reason there is a revelatory glass-ceiling within the church is because Main Street has been contained by God-imposed limits of understanding about the kingdom. This containment serves two purposes; it limits the clown's power and simultaneously entices the people.

In other words, He only wants you to experience a certain amount of revelation through the emissaries. He only gives messengers enough to whet the appetite of the community. His desire is that the individual come to Him and eat at His table. If God removed the spiritual containment - the glass ceiling - authentic leaders would naturally become something inappropriate to the people in much larger measure that we see today. Similarly, if He removed the glass ceiling, the clown would inherit a much greater degree of power over the encampment. His perfect plan would cease to exist.

New eyes not only helped assure my true identity, enable me to diagnose kingdom wrongs and prompt greater levels of spiritual discernment, they also showed me why I needed to repent. Most leaders are guilty of presenting a pink message, but people like me who place them on a pedestal are truly the ones to blame. I can thrash, kick, and indict all day long because of the ongoing falsities of bad leadership, but I accomplish nothing if I don't acknowledge my role and responsibility in their ordination.

Put another way, a guy like Al Sharpton can complain about the injustices of the leading race in America until he is blue in the face, but his legitimate points are lost when he fails to acknowledge his own contribution to the race problem in America.

The further I advance through the mountain the more truth is illuminated. New eyes are a wonderful gift but they have also burdened my conscience with somber humility. His heart for the inhabitants of the IDP camp burns with such passion that to try and look with new eyes at it is akin to a piano being dropped on my chest.

He'll do anything, and he's done everything, for the hope of spending one magical candlelit dinner with you. Intellectually speaking I've known this to be true for some time, but new eyes are what give my heart a reason to ache.

Taking Back Ground

Chapter 11 – Addiction

It's time to start taking back spiritual ground. The best way to do that is by learning to abide not in this world but in an eternal dwelling place. This chapter will center on addictive behavior as a result of unhealthy alliances with the clown.

You're not crazy. Sounds trivial, right? It isn't. I can't tell you how many times I've heard people say, "do you think I'm crazy?"

No, you're not crazy, but don't ask the clown. He's intent on convincing you that you are.

The world of psychotherapy is a multibillion dollar industry because so many people have come to believe that they are nuts. This is another in a long line of tactics the clown has used to try and numb the church to a pink apathy. If he succeeds in making us believe that we *need* drugs or medication to cope with stress, he has won a huge victory.

Chaos thrives in the company of the clown. The clown dances around the room with bells, whistles, gongs and elaborate outfits to try and draw our attention. He knows that if you're focused on him, you're not focused on Christ. He's fast. He can whip around a room faster than our eyes can track, and if we're concerned with what the clown is doing, we're gonna get dizzy. When we get dizzy, we throw up. When we vomit we start believing that indeed, we may be going insane.

It's impossible to know how much of our physical illness correlates directly back to spiritual chaos, but the older I get the more I'm convinced physicality is profoundly tied to spiritual chaos.

The world's response to the dancing, whirling clown is to prescribe psychotropic medication which numbs our ability to care about what he's doing. Though medication makes us feel better, it also corrupts our ability to care about what Christ is doing. Addiction is the coping skill of the apathetic.

If you find yourself relying heavily on drugs to cope with life this chapter may be hard to read. Psychotropic meds do help make life tolerable in the short-term, and I've seen their effectiveness time and again in the Health and Human Services industry. Taking medication is not a sin, but an issue arises when we become addicted and the medication becomes a crutch. Everything from painkillers to sleeping pills to mood stabilizers (both the legal and illegal variety), when we rely on the drug to help us cope with a certain element of life we effectively reject Christ's desire to bring comfort. Like stress eating, we choose to rely on a horizontal remedy as opposed to the vertical one.

This section of the book is about taking back spiritual ground. Taking back spiritual ground is never easy. It can be painful. Kicking an addiction is never comfortable but it is necessary, however, to pursue Christ's direction with regard to usage if we ever hope to experience Him in fullness. Like any 12-step program will tell you, kicking addiction starts with honesty.

There is a misnomer in the pink church, that if something is hard it must also be bad. It is especially true in the west where luxuries and comforts abound. We value comforts and happiness, and seek to attain them at the expense of what may be better for us or more appropriate. It's not a hard and fast rule, but my experience has told me that living life in lockstep with Christ is often harder, especially in the beginning, than living without Him. He asks us to do things that are good for us, but aren't necessarily easy. He asks us to shake off the alliances we've made with the clown, but those alliances are often comforting. He asks us to let Him impart freedom, but it takes a tremendous amount of faith and trust to believe that He will uphold his promise.

Whether talking about loosening the bonds of addiction or dispensing with other alliances we've made with the clown, the process of delving into the mountain is always going to be a challenge. We are assured of this in Scripture.

But beyond the assurance of challenge, there is a silver lining best articulated in James 1:2-4. It says, *"Count it all joy, my brothers, when you meet trials of various kinds, for you know that the testing of your faith produces steadfastness.* ***And let steadfastness have its full effect, that you may be perfect and complete, lacking in nothing."***

I try not to look at life's decisions in the context of hard versus easy anymore. I try to make decisions based on whether or not I'm in alignment with truth. It is a lie to believe that medication is required sustenance to cope with life. Very few people are truly in this category, yet the vast majority of addicts behave as though their life depended on their drug.

I'm not advocating for anyone to throw their medication out the window or flush it down the toilet, but I am trying to relay the importance of placing your medication on its appropriate shelf in your life. In the most prominent spot on the center of your mantelpiece Christ must reign supreme. Medicine may or may not be an appropriate additive to your life, but if it is, it needs to be in the medicine cabinet where it belongs and not in a place of prominence.

The only way to know if your medication is an appropriate additive is to put it on the altar and let Christ convict you one way or the other. But when you put it on the altar, you must be willing to let it go if He tells you to. There is no hard and fast rule for everybody, but if medication has become your lifeblood, be prepared for a profound increase in your level of courage and sagacity as you traverse the next section of the mountain. It is my experience that He intends to rip dependence off us to make way for a life fully dependent on Him.

We take back spiritual ground when we agree with truth and shun the lie that tells us to rely on things other than Christ to cope with stress. If Christ is not allowed to help us cope with stress, we have rejected his Lordship in our lives. We have rejected intimacy.

Pink

Is this to say you can't take drugs if you're living in the mountain? No, I'm not saying that at all. But the problem with pink Christians is that they've never let Christ vet their medication use and consequently, it's become an addiction. The pink are notorious for swallowing (no pun intended) whatever the Doctor orders. And I use the word "Doctor" very loosely.

If you struggle with uncertainty about how to dispense with certain sinful alliances, I have a recommendation. It has to do with a little tactic I used back in the day (and still do sometimes) that helped wean me off of the clown's rusty hooks.

Dedicate quality time not quantity-time, every day, to intentionally pursuing your right identity in Christ. It can be as little as 10 minutes. I've never met someone who could not dedicate 10 minutes of their day to something, so hopefully you are not the first.

During that time it's important to leave your house or office. You don't have to go far, but you should get outside the confines of your regular routine. You can sit on a porch, in the backyard, in the front yard, in a park or even your car. Getting out of the home or office automatically triggers your mind that a transition has occurred, and you will minimize the distractions significantly. Don't take your cell phone. Don't listen to music. Don't take a book. We're only talking about 10 minutes here.

Assign that place as your sanctuary, your mountain spot. Go to that place and sit down. Don't pray, don't fold your hands or bow your head, just sit. Take in the sounds of life around you. Take in the silence. Hear the birds. Take a few deep breaths and calm down.

Once you are calm, close your eyes and imagine yourself walking into your eternal dwelling place or into the throne room of heaven, or maybe just the front door of the mountain ablaze with the manifest presence of God. Just imagine it, and feel free to make it up as you go. Use your imagination. Notice the contour of the walls, how the lights hang. Are the lights even hanging? Maybe the light comes from inside the brick-and-mortar structure? Is there water? Is there a river? What does the sky look like? While you're in that place, be willing to really let your imagination go.

The place you are imagining is a place that's better than the world that's got you tied up in knots. This place you are imagining is the manifestation of everything you know to be good and true and real about God. Let your mind explore that place. Leave the IDP camp behind and imagine yourself taking a journey into an eternal spiritual place that is all your own.

When you open your eyes you will be more relaxed. When you open your eyes you're gonna feel less stressed. Visualization is not that uncommon; this is a tactic often prescribed in the world of psychotherapy. But a reduction to your stress is not the point. The point wasn't to teach you a new coping skill that helps you better enjoy a life of rape and battery with the clown. The point of this exercise goes much deeper.

When you align yourself with Christ by visualizing His abode according to the truths you know, you are actually leaving the realm of psychiatric visualization and entering a spiritual communion with Jesus. It's not good enough to imagine Cozumel and a Corona Light, you actually have to build this world in your mind based on truth.

Example, *God is all-powerful.* Okay. So, in your mind, what is representative of all-encompassing power? Maybe it's a mountain, maybe it's an ocean, and maybe it's something completely different. Visualize that.

In another example, *Jesus loves me*. Great. Now in your mind, what represents pure love? Is it representative of someone building you an eternal dwelling? Is it representative of someone holding you, caring for you, valuing you for who you are? Is it representative of someone protecting you? You get to build the world, have fun with it!

How about the truth that, *your value can never be measured by your works?* What does that look like? Maybe that truth is represented by angels flying around and catering to your every need? Or maybe it's represented by unfettered access to an amazing dinner party, high up in the upper echelon of the mountain.

By building manifest truth in your imagination, you are actually interacting with Christ. This is how we meditate on His goodness. In this world you're not thinking about popping a pill to cope. Your to-do list does not exist. In this world you're putting definitions to the truth of what it means to be freely loved by Christ Jesus. I assure you, it's better than drugs.

10 minutes a day. Best 10 minutes you could ever spend.

In the beginning this place will be your imaginary sanctuary, but as you construct the manifestation of truth, you'll no longer be cutting 10 minutes out of your life to engage with Jesus, you'll be cutting 1,430 minutes out of your day to live in the temporal world. This is because Christ will meet you there, and the place of imagination will become more real to you than the walls and ceiling of your earthly abode.

This is taking back spiritual ground. This is a tangible exercise on how to shun the clown's lies and choose instead to abide in Christ. As you dedicate 10 minutes each day to this activity, you'll learn how to seamlessly go in and out of your kingdom of abode regardless of what's going on around you. You won't have to find a quiet spot and calm yourself down, you'll learn to engage Him amidst the chaos and filth of the IDP camp.

For my life, having made it a point to do this little exercise for years, I've come to live in the spiritual dwelling more easily than I do in the physical one. Am I crazy? No. I'm not crazy, but this is my reality and it's the greatest reality I've ever known.

Chapter 12 - Carnage on the Home Front

Based on Scripture, here is a peek into a day in the life of Zechariah:

"Eliza! I require your assistance, my dear!"

Confound this stupid Ephod, he thought. *Today of all days, why can I not seem to get this girdle…*

"ELIZA! Come now, as I have asked!"

In desperation, the old man's fingers worked along the broad length of the harness that held the ephod in place. Though very familiar with the priestly regalia, on this particular day he'd become bemused by its many clasps and ties. Little beads of sweat splashed into his eyes and dove off the hook of his nose. His breath came in hushed gasps through clenched teeth as his arthritic fingers worked to reverse his mistake.

He grunted and blinked as sweat stung the corners of his eyes. Exasperated the old priest stomped his foot, ready to howl a third time for his wife when she burst into the room.

"Zechariah," she gasped, "good gracious."

She hurried to lend him a hand, assessing his predicament as she crossed the room.

"The time is late, and here, you have not even begun to assemble the *choshen*…"

She knelt down next to him and took over. Her hands were more fluid and it only took a second before she'd identified his mistake. She glanced up at her elderly husband, wondering about senility.

"The damn thing has fussed on this day that I was *selected* to perform the incense ritual. That Hezekim, I'm sure he became ill. He could not have given me notice of more than a quarter of the sun risen day…"

Zechariah suspended his rant to take a passionate swipe at an abject fly. As he did, he lost his balance and slugged into his wife. She fell back and caught herself before casting an incensed look at her husband. Together they fell head-first into a swirling pit of chaos.

The fly dodged his swipe and continued to bat this way and that, beating in perfect harmony to the symphony of chaos and hysteria in Zechariah's mind. Reassuming her crouched position, Eliza thrust her shoulder back and tugged at a knot, this time causing him to teeter. The two looked at one another, flashing deep crevices of frustration. It was a stalemate moment.

He looked away and resumed mumbling as she recommenced her work on his regalia.

She was a perceptive and discerning woman, and noticed the obscenities rattling around his mutterings. Frustration was common but obscenity was not. Though his words upset her she decided to hold her tone. This was neither the place nor the time for a scolding, but the way in which he carried on was very uncharacteristic.

As if recognizing her offenses, his mumblings became louder. It was as though some unseen spirit was trying to bait her into scolding him so as to drive a wedge between them. She knew the spirit, and having identified it she realized how she needed to respond.

Fighting back her own agitation she forced her softest and most empathetic tone. "Now Zechariah *Kohen*, let us not become flippant with the tongue, but remember to give the utmost of reverence to Him who creates, who has given and multiplied, who has shown…"

"Shown us the abundance of peace and joy in a life of servitude," he finished, disparagement oozing forth.

In that moment something happened. He felt a sharp pang on his heart and realized his own shameful behavior. He cast a glance down toward his wife, who returned it with a look of disapproval, though unable to hide the deep and profound love she felt for him. Even in his most immature moments of passion, by God, she still loved him.

After undoing the wrongly woven strands of the Ephod she paused and grabbed hold of a piece of cloth lying at her husband's feet. While tightly grasping hold of her work along the lower-left torso of her 5'5" spouse, she handed the cloth up to him and said, "Wipe down your forehead, love, speak with thanksgiving in the moments when it is difficult and feel the peace in your heart once again."

What wisdom, he thought.

Emotions justified his anger but his intellect knew better. She was right. All he needed to do was take a deep breath, stop entertaining the negative thoughts in his mind, and remember that God is in control. The synagogue leaders would fret and cast condescending looks in his direction when he arrived late for the ritual, but how was that any different from their normal demeanor toward him?

Really, he thought, *what am I so worried about? The ritual will start when I arrive.*

Just as he was beginning to relax he thought about the planned activity he'd be missing out on tonight. He was looking forward to a cool evening under the fig trees, drinking a glass of wine and watching his nieces and nephews play. After all, hanging out with family was why he and his wife had come to Jerusalem early.

He felt himself losing control again. Peace was beginning to evaporate. He felt the justified anger welling up in his chest and locked his knees in frustration. As the emotions justified negativity, and the negativity churned like fresh dough in his mind, he lost the clarity he had only seconds earlier enjoyed.

Oh yes, he reinforced quietly, *I certainly do have cause to be angry! Instead of spending time with my relatives, I inherit the responsibility of another priest!*

He was in jeopardy of cycling back into chaotic anger again when he noticed his wife. She was whispering something, a prayer? He couldn't tell. He did however recognize that she was still selflessly working on his clothes, and that was enough.

He pushed the ranting aside and bit his lip. She was right and he knew it. His attitude toward the circumstance was not making the situation any better. In fact, it was making it worse.

It is not as though my grumbling is going to make Hezekim uphold his God-sanctioned duties... he finally conceded.

Zechariah suddenly went on the spiritual offensive and was well on his way to winning the battle in his mind. He used the cloth she handed him and dabbed his forehead with it. As he did, he took a few forced deep breaths and finally exhaled, exclaiming almost inaudibly, "God is good."

Oh the power in three little words.

At that very instant, a pale breeze swept into the little hut through the window-hole and carried with it the fragrance of wildflowers.

Elizabeth suspended her work – she had to – the climate change was so overt. He looked down at her and watched as she tilted her head back, eyes shut, donning a slight curve of contentment upon her mouth. She breathed deeply, taking in the clean air that suddenly seemed to live in the high-priest's guesthouse.

His heart rate slowed to a more human pace as the breeze cooled his sweat-drenched skin. He too took a deep breath, this time not to force calmness, but to inhale peace.

Oftentimes carnage on the home front is nothing more than bad emotional justification and an abject fly buzzing around. I obviously made up the details of the story but is it so hard to imagine? Is it so unlike the things we experience, especially in a run-up to something wonderful?

If you've read Scripture, you know that on this particular day Zechariah was going to receive a visitation from an Archangel. God was going to give him a message about the coming birth of his son. Had he known the day would turn out to be so magnificent, would he have been so quick to anger? I doubt it. But we lack the gift of foresight. Foresight robs us of our need for Christ, so rather than foresight He gave us faith.

Foresight notwithstanding, the clown does have a funny way of sniffing these things out ahead of time. He has a cunning way of identifying the coming blessing and lambasting us in the season prior. If I've experienced it once, I've experienced it 100 times; a season of turmoil followed by a windfall of revelation and blessing.

Bucking an emotional justification takes courage, but recognizing the need to buck it takes sagacity. In this story, suitably, it was Elizabeth's sagacious wisdom that brought truth to Zechariah, and his courage that put truth into effect. In their sagaciously courageous response to an array of circumstantial frustrations, the voice of the enemy was neutralized by their decision to align with Christ in saying, *God is good*.

My wife and I use the phrase, "letting the enemy in". It's how we articulate the meddling of the clown. The clown's authority to exert voodoo in my home is restricted by virtue of our (my wife and my) partnership with truth. It's when we either individually or as a couple begin to partner with a lie, that we in effect "let the enemy in" our home. The clown's ability to upset your peace corresponds directly to your choice of partnership.

This can get maddening. Sometimes the clown tells you that you're justified in being angry at someone, and he's absolutely right. You are justified. But justification does not correspond to truth, and just because you're justified doesn't mean you have to partner with a lie. Christ was justified in asking God to take the cup of sorrow from Him prior to his murder, but he was right to not demand it.

This is a fundamental aspect of spiritual warfare. The enemy uses things like circumstance and feelings to tempt us into justifying a corrosive response. Because in another era of our lives the clown was successful in convincing us that the world is somehow fair, we feel further anchored in our unhealthy justification. But when we choose to live vertically in firm submission to Christ, we forego a certain set of conditioned responses - not on the basis of justification - but on the basis of truth.

In a game of poker, truth is always the royal flush while a lie can be any hand but the royal flush. If you partner with truth you always have a winning hand. If we have a hard time allowing truth to supersede justification, we have not progressed very far into the mountain.

I've found that carnage on the home front can often be averted by adopting a few basic spiritual warfare principles.

First, agree that the clown's access to you and your family

is not a matter of his right, but a matter of his permission. Ultimately, God permits what God permits. But in the context of God's permissive will, the clown only has the right to wreak havoc if you give him permission. You're the gatekeeper. You give or deny the clown access to your family and relationships based on your partnership.

Second, the moment you recognize that an evil principality is at work in your home, agree with me that you have the authority to dismiss it. It may try to resist, and in my experience it normally does, but ultimately it lacks the authority to stay if you've established that it is unwelcome. You establish that it is unwelcome by affirming your alignment, in speech and/or deed, with truth.

Finally, agree that you will let the enemy in from time to time. It's part of being human. As such, if a loved one is calling you out and says "I think you're letting the enemy in," you ought to be able to take a step back and analyze that assessment for what it is. If you can't, or if you find yourself emotionally outraged at the insinuation, your spouse's point has just been vindicated. This truth cuts both ways, husband to wife as well as wife to husband.

Wherever you are in the mountain, near the entry point or

deep in its bowels, spotting principalities of darkness are easy once you get the hang of it. There is a difference between someone being upset and in genuine need of a hug, and someone being upset and justifying a cutting and mean-spirited attitude. The difference between those two things is that the latter has the clown's fingerprints all over it and should not be allowed to stand.

Sagacity informs us, courage enables us, and when despite our best efforts we fail and screw things up, Christ is the one who perfects all things.

Closing your eyes and hoping that truth prevails amidst the clown's menacing tactics is different from opening your eyes, sticking your finger in his eye, and making a declaration of truth with your audible voice. In the context of spiritual warfare, there's a big difference between hope that Christ will intervene on your behalf, and laying hold of the kingdom by declaring the authority you already possess in Him.

Christ declared that all authority in heaven and earth has been given to Him, and He has endowed that authority to the coheirs of the kingdom - you and I. By hoping for His intervention in the midst of the enemy's attack, you effectively relinquish the authority you already possess. By declaring truth and silencing the enemy where he stands, you effectively partner with the authority you already possess.

Application: I'm having a really bad day and the whispers of deceit are telling me that I'm a failure at work, as a father, and as a husband. I'm being turned like a top, and I begin to lose my way. Piggybacking on the lie that has assaulted me all morning, I begin to believe that I'm a terrible writer and unfit to deliver the message God called me to. Frustrated, I take it out on my wife by isolating and watching TV, and I bark at my kids for having the audacity to play boisterously in my presence.

Sadly, this scenario is not all that uncommon for me and it may not be uncommon for you. This is precisely how the clown meddles in my psyche. Sometimes it's a few minutes before I recognize it. Other times I'll go days under the heavy weight of frustration and spiritual confusion. Even after I identify the root of my struggle, I sometimes choose to stay there because misery loves company, and I have found solace in my own depressive attitude.

Once I identify the root cause, I then have to make a choice to partner with truth. It's worth noting that, even if the root cause remains evasive and goes undetected, I can still partner with truth and end the misery. Sometimes it's the hardest thing I've ever tried to do because the enemy has his hooks in me so deep.

But once I so choose Him, I courageously stand up and articulate some variation of the words, "Clown, by the authority vested in me through Jesus Christ, I choose to reestablish my firm identity in Him and you are no longer welcome here."

Sometimes the clown gets slapped so hard he flees. Other times, he lingers and chooses to give me another hard right hook. If he lingers, sometimes I'll walk through my house praying in the spirit. Sometimes I'll mock him, and remind him that he's a defeated weakling.

Sometimes I'll just reiterate the truth statement from above and follow that up with, "Now I've told you twice. Stick around at your own peril, but I'm gonna keep on kicking your ass until I get tired, and when you crawl back into your hole, I'm going to write another chapter in Pink Christianity and by God, may it serve to firebomb your encampment! You're messin' with the wrong guy, you little gremlin."

Chapter 13 - Carnage on the Inside

The other day my three-year-old started crying for no apparent reason. If you have kids, you know this is not uncommon. But intuition on this occasion told me that something was wrong. I asked her why she was crying. She caught enough composure to say, "Because I don't make you proud."

Some may look at a situation like this and say, "Where did that come from?" or "Honey, of course I'm proud of you! Why on earth would you say such a thing?"

With sincerity we'd rack our brains, recounting every nuance of the recent engagements trying to identify where we might have inadvertently transmitted that message. *Did I fail to acknowledge her for something? Did my body language convey that I was disappointed in her for something? …*

Confused, we'd scoop the child up and affirm the contrary, and tell her in no uncertain terms how extremely proud she makes her daddy. Maybe she'd believe it and maybe not. But if this was the extent of my response, all I'd have managed to do is enter a shouting match with a nefarious character who happens to possess a stronger voice and needs no breaks.

I've spent enough time in the mountain to know a thing or two about the enemy and my eyes have been opened to the clown's deceit. In my spirit I knew exactly where her deception came from, but it wasn't important that I could peg it. What's important is that she learns how to identify it.

As soon as she uttered those words, I stopped whatever I was doing and picked her up into my lap. I chose not to start off with, "Oh Ari, of course I'm proud of you!" Instead, I looked my three-year-old square in the eyes and I asked her to tell me, "Who told you that I'm not proud of you?"

Her response was, and I quote, "A Grinch came to me in my dream and told me that you're not proud of me…"

The clown was in my daughter's bedroom. Even worse, he was in her mind. She's only three, or was at the time of this incident.

Self-hatred is the root of all sorts of carnage on the inside. What better way to make a child hate herself than to convince her that she is a disappointment? Where do you suppose kids learn how to convince themselves that they are not the apple of their daddy's eye? Where do you think children learn how to lie, steal, and cheat? In some cases, they learn these things from the derelicts that raise them. But if it was all a result of parenting many youngsters would surely not have to wrestle with the onset of self-loathing, and as far as I know, every person struggles with this. I can honestly say I've never known a single person in my life who hasn't wrestled with self-hatred at one level or another.

Be it daytime or nighttime, the sleepless clown is always hard at work in the minds of our little ones. I'm certain he starts this lifelong assault the moment a child is conceived. Even in the mother's womb, he's poking and prodding; he's doing everything in his power to convince little ones to hate themselves. This is a tactical decision on his part. If he can teach children to hate themselves, then he can paint God however he so desires and easily convince the self-hater of his painting's authenticity.

If he does a good job when they're young, his job is easier when they grow up. The clown doesn't fight fair, the clown fights to win. If enough carnage is spun; if enough self-hatred is believed, the person will be hard-pressed to ever find his/her way out of the maze. And I submit that without Christ, no one would ever experience the sweet taste of freedom outside the clown's labyrinth of despair.

As parents what can we do? How do we defend our children against a predator that we cannot see? What are the warfare principles that apply in a situation such as this? Though it is not simple there is an answer, and it begins with, *in the event of an emergency, oxygen masks will drop from the overhead compartments.* **First strap on your mask** *and then assist those around you…*

Parents have a hard time shielding their kids from the clown's lies because they have not mastered the ability to shield themselves. Most parents fight spiritual battles with guilt and shame. Most children end up watching their parents use guilt and shame, and all this does is further ingrain the enemy's lie. It's a vicious cycle.

In spiritual warfare, *strapping on the oxygen mask* is the act of cleaning out the carnage from within ourselves. I'm certain there are many ways in which to journey this path of healing with Christ, but all I can tell you about is my journey. Though my journey will be unique in some ways, I think the broader strokes apply to just about everybody.

At one of those points in the maturation process, a good mile or two inside the mountain, I came to a dark and lonely cavern in the terrain. My throat was parched, my stomach grumbled with hunger. It was uncomfortable and to make matters worse, Jesus was off doing something else. I was alone and afraid.

In my mind I heard the whispers of deceit tell me that I had been abandoned. I looked around, and circumstances appeared to support the accusation. I had to do something. I had to get out of this frightening canyon.

One hand in front of the other, I began to climb the cliff to try and reach higher ground. As I climbed, the fog thickened and got to the point that I could barely see the handholds in the rock. To make matters worse, the air was moist and cold and my fingers were losing their agility. The whispers of deceit told me I'd fall, and that I could never reach the destinations I set for myself. I was exhausted, my fingers were numb and all around me was thick fog. Once again, the circumstance supported the accusation.

Muscles aching, I forced myself to take another step and grab another hold in the rock-face. I had no way of knowing how much further it was to the top, but I had to try. I needed to try and prove the clown wrong. Scared, I kept climbing.

20 minutes later the air began to clear and my sight returned. Hopeful, I looked up to try and glimpse the top. But as the clouds evaporated and pulled away from the cliff all I saw was more rock. My heart sank. *There is no way I'm gonna reach the top. It's just too far…*

As if cued by the conductor of an orchestra, the whispers of deceit returned. "If you were worth saving, your God would have made this cliff manageable. As it is, He's left you here to die."

Another step followed by another grip, and suddenly I slipped. Unable to catch myself, I fell back into the thick white fog below. In my mind rang the echo of laughter and mockery. The clown appeared to have won.

His cackle faded from my mind just as my downward speed slowed and then stopped altogether. I was hovering like a helicopter, suspended in the air. Something, or *someone* had a hold of my hand. Then I realized we were not hovering at all but ascending. I was passing the rock face that I had fallen off of, and soon we burst through the cloud again and I was back in the clear air. I looked, and holding onto my hand was Jesus.

We ascended all the way to the top and touched down on the neon green turf of a beautiful field. A lazy river snaked its way through the rocks and I could hear the chirps and clicks of animal life. The sights were colorful and bright. I never heard the whispers of deceit denigrate my character again, and somewhere in the back of my mind I sometimes wonder what happened to that stupid laugh, so full of feigned assurance. *Who's laughing now?*

The Lord dealt with my inner carnage through my own futile attempts to deal with it the best way I knew how. You may know this to be true, but fear, apprehension, self-hatred, envy, and all forms of other spiritual gangrene really begin to manifest when you're doing things that confront their base of strength.

If you're a person who struggles with irrational fear, and you choose to confront it by, say, taking a walk in the dark, you'll stir the spirit up. It will posture and attempt to convince you that your efforts are futile and it will assure you that you're in danger. All sorts of thoughts and crazy nightmarish contingencies will flash through your mind because the clown doesn't want you to confront his base of strength in your life.

Pink

I think it's important, so I'm going to jot down a few examples of this. Keep in mind, though these examples may seem extremely superficial to some, the principality is equally crippling whether based in a superficial or profound premise.

The first example: A mid-20s gal who is wildly self-conscious about some element of her looks. Let's say she's self-conscious about her legs. When she goes shopping, she's always looking for a cute outfit that will mask her legs. Everywhere she goes, regardless of the temperature, she's wearing jeans or other variations of long pants. Once in a while, she'll suffer the capris, but not very often.

The act of climbing the cliff - or putting on the oxygen mask during an aeronautical crisis - comes when she sees a pair of shorts that she loves, buys them, and chooses to wear them to the park with her friends. To a person who struggles with this, everything about the idea of buying shorts and wearing them out in public is nauseating and can even bring an onset of physical illness.

Why are issues of self-consciousness such a big deal? Because intimacy is garnered through vulnerability and vulnerability is, in essence, nakedness. Total transparency. It's impossible to get to know the heart of God who will demand every piece of you if you can't even wear shorts in public.

Another example. Say Jenny is deathly afraid of the dark. Because of this, she refuses to stay in a house alone for even a single night. When you ask Jenny why she's so afraid of the dark, she might say that she had a lot of nightmares as a child. Maybe something happened during nighttime that caused trauma, or maybe she's just convinced that the bogeyman is out to get her. Fear is immobility, and immobility stifles the journey into the mountain.

Jenny hates her fear, but she can't bring herself to confront the whispers of deceit when they tell her that something bad will happen if she chooses to take a walk at night. But she hates her fear, so she puts on her shoes and coat, and opens the front door. It's a nice night. She works up the nerve to set out and makes it to the sidewalk, hangs a left, and begins to walk down the block.

Hey, this isn't so bad, she thinks, and just as she does the whisper of deceit calls her attention to the bark of a dog in the distance. The clown says "did you hear that? That dog is not in a yard. The barks are getting louder. I think he's coming up here, coming for you…"

Jenny stops moving, panics and strains her ears hoping to either confirm or deny the clown's assessment. Indeed, the dog does sound like it's coming closer, the barks are getting louder. Once again she's petrified and immobile.

Whether she pushes onward or turns around in this very moment is a really big deal, spiritually. This moment of decision is akin to my moment on the cliff. *Should I start climbing down or do I push onward?*

By pushing onward, she partners with truth and places her trust in God for protection. This is what we call "trust well-placed". But by turning around, she's putting her trust in the fear-mongering clown's assertion of potential danger. This is called "trust misplaced". The decision is black or white, either she partners with truth or she partners with a lie.

Why is irrational fear such a clown-favorite tool of spiritual warfare? Because the mountain is intimidating. God is intimidating. He's higher and deeper and wider than anything we could ever imagine, and if we are afraid of His true nature, then it's impossible to place our trust in Him when it comes to issues of protection, or anything else.

Final example. George is a husky guy who overeats when he gets stressed. Maybe George was an abuse victim growing up, or maybe his parents simply set poor examples. Regardless of where the partnership was made, George is bound in chains by virtue of the fact that his go-to response to stress is food. He's realizing this about himself, but he's addicted and can't seem to shake his need for the comfort that food brings, especially in moments of stress.

George hates that he relies on food for stress mitigation so he decides to fast and pray. But before the fast even begins, he's inundated with the clown's deceit… "You're an unhealthy guy with bad cholesterol, a fast will be bad for you." … "If you try fasting and don't make it through, you'll be worse off than you are today."

In defiance of the deceit, George decides to start his fast, and typical to form, something happens that stresses him out. He's told that he failed his recent midterm. Knowing that his angry and abusive father is going to have a field day over this, he immediately reaches for a candy bar.

What George decides to do in that moment is of paramount importance. Either he chooses to self-soothe with food and seek a temporary solution to an eternal problem, or he decides to walk into the open arms of Christ and be comforted in a new and foreign, but lasting way.

The reason that stress eating is so debilitating is because it limits a person's ability to experience the comfort of the Lord. If we never experience comfort from the Lord, the clown easily paints God as unemotional and aloof. Even something as superficial as stress eating is an insurmountable barrier between George and the one who loves him the most, because George never fully experiences love, and therefore could never fully experience God in truth.

There are a million other examples I could give of spiritual principalities that leave carnage all over our insides. They can be as superficial as "I hate the shape of my hips" or as profound as "I can't open up in relationships because I'm afraid of being hurt". Every person is unique and each must ultimately discover which principalities they have aligned with. The best way to discover this is to launch from point A straight to B, then C, and keep going straight through the mountain.

I find that identification is sometimes the hardest part. Once you identify what the principality is, the act of dealing with it is not difficult at all. Sure, it'll take a little courage, but it's not difficult when you force yourself to realize that the clown's words are hollow and empty and categorically false.

In the example I gave of my own journey, I was trying to get through a real crux in the path of healing. I knew I wanted to get to a higher place in the mountain, somewhere less depressing and isolative. When I started challenging my fears, the clown whispered deceit to try and overpower me by the principality that I'd aligned with in my youth. In my example above, it's clear I was struggling with the fear of abandonment and the fear of failure.

But by pushing through and continuing to climb, I effectively rejected the partnership I had made with the clown and established a new partnership with Christ. We don't necessarily have cliffs to climb, but the way this plays out is as follows:

First, we identify the principality, and that becomes clear as we delve into the mountain. In this step people can be a great resource. Find somebody who knows you really well and has some wisdom in Christ, and ask them to help guide you into areas of your past where partnerships became established.

If you don't have the luxury of a Spirit-filled friend, you

don't need one. I didn't have one for much of my journey either. In those times I asked the Lord a simple question, "God, why am I the way I am?"

On the heels of that question I began writing, and out of those journal entries came my first book, *Pathways to Abandon*. Writing is a powerful way to express what's going on inside. While you're alone with the Lord, ask Him to reveal stuff about your past. Give Him permission to search your heart's partnerships and illuminate them.

However you attempt to identify the principality, if you truly desire to know, you'll know. Jesus made you a promise in Matthew 7:7 when He said, "Ask, and it will be given to you; seek, and you will find; knock, and it will be opened to you…"

Next, you confront the principality by doing exactly the opposite of whatever it's trying to convince you of. If it's fear-based, put your trust in Christ and march into the lion's den. If the principality is rooted in self-abasement, start proclaiming the truth about your beauty to Christ, and to your friends and family. Make a conscientious lifestyle change.

Third, when the principality rears up in anger toward your defiance of it, push through. That *push through* part often looks like verbal pronouncement - as opposed to physical rock-climbing - and similar to the explanation given in the previous chapter about Zechariah. If it's fear you're dealing with and the enemy rears up and tries to scare you, open your mouth and say out loud, "Christ will never leave me or forsake me, whom shall I fear?"

You see, the *push through* step has everything to do with a conscientious decision. It is identical to what Jesus did during His 40-day desert experience. There is no difference. The clown/Satan will regularly try and convince you of his perspective, and the only way to not align yourself with his perspective is to defy it with a conscientious choice to the contrary. In the case of Jenny, she could either defy Satan by verbally making an assertion like the one above, "Christ will never leave me nor forsake me, whom shall I fear" or she can just choose to keep walking straight into the sound of that dog's bark. Either way, the new partnership has been established. The partnership with fear (a lie) has been broken, and the partnership with safety in Christ (truth) has been established.

This is where it gets fun. Once you defy the clown, something magical happens.

Pink

You'll notice that I never made it to the end of my journey; I never made it to the top of that cliff. Oftentimes, the manifestation of this spiritual war in the physical is not what we supposed it would be. It is my experience that Jesus will never miss an opportunity to establish himself as Lord and Savior in my life. Climbing the cliff was not just about bucking and overturning a spiritual partnership, it was also about getting high enough up that in the end I'd lose my grip and fall. I had to place all my trust in Christ Jesus in order to clear the carnage from the inside. It would not have been enough for me to take another four or five steps in defiance of the whispers of deceit, and then turn around and climb down to safety. I needed to go until exhaustion got the better of me because in that moment Christ knew he had me forever.

You can't confront your historical partnerships half-assed. Well, you can, but you will not succeed in breaking them. You must persevere and go all the way. You have to defy mortality and pursue well past the point of no return. I say *defy mortality* because this pursuit will take you well past the fears you have of temporal circumstances and even mortal death.

I said this part is fun. It's fun because it's exhilarating when you cannot fail. Why? Because He cannot fail and He cannot lie. If you choose to go all the way in defiance of mortality, then you will experience for the first time in your life, a *sure thing*. I know of no other way to experience a sure thing in this life outside of placing everything I have in Christ.

Once we allow Christ to do a changing work in our lives, the carnage of our past associations dissipates. As the carnage dissipates, the eyes open up. As the eyes open up we inherit increased measures of wisdom in truth, and are able to begin managing the clown's assaultive tendencies in the lives of our children.

Parents, it is not good enough for you to get into a shouting match with the clown and try to compete for your child's attention in that venue. The clown will win this battle every time. You need to articulate truth in a way that is tangible and understandable, and start teaching your kids the skills needed to ward off the onslaught. Good habits learned at a young age will pay great dividends as they grow. If you can convince your children that their inheritance is in the kingdom of heaven, and that their protection, provision, identity and assurances are all wrapped up in their willingness to partner with truth, even at the age of three they will confound the enemy to no end.

I regularly remind my children that they have authority

over the Grinch that shows up in their nightmares. I tell them that when they feel scared, they can always speak the name of Jesus and defy their fears. They know about the love of the Father, and how it overcomes fear when they choose to partner with truth.

While they are small, the responsibility is incumbent on the parent to spiritually guard and protect their young from the clown. Covering your kids in prayer, speaking out declarations of truth in their bedroom at night, and living a life of joy and peace before them are the most fundamental things a parent can do. As they get a little older and develop an ability to reason for themselves, I encourage you to begin showing them how to defend themselves against evil in their own prayer life. When the clown slithers in, let your child experience the power of a declaration. Hold their hand, go through that darkness with them, the let the child know what it feels like to wield the authority of the kingdom of heaven.

When they are able to identify the enemy's fingerprints in the lives of their friends, start showing them how to defend the ones they love. Tell them how to edify their friends with words of affirmation and declarations of truth. Speaking truth does not make your child a geek, it just makes him/her the only kid in the region who possesses confidence and self-assurance uncommon to the human experience.

By defending children against the falsities of self-disparagement when they are young, we in effect defend them against dangerous temptations and reckless pursuits when they become adolescents as well. This is not to say that our children won't struggle in life, because they will. Everyone struggles. This is not to say that they will not hit a rock-bottom somewhere down the road, because I'm sure they will. Without a rock-bottom, it's hard to define what it is we are forgiven for, and harder still to fully appreciate what it is we are offered in Christ. But equipping your children for the war is just good sense and it has the potential of saving them from a lot of anguish in the long run.

Chapter 14 - Isolating in Shame

Sin is a bugaboo for the pink. People who live in the IDP camp are, if they are honest, regularly confounded by sin because they can never fully get their arms around it. Most try to manage it and keep certain realities about their sin-life locked up in the basement. Some toss their hands up, kick the dirt, and let sleeping dogs lie. I've done both.

Before I found tent-city, sin did not matter. I lived like a heathen and pushed away any sense of guilt, shame or conviction. I chose to not to dwell on my own poor behavior because I was too interested in experiencing the world and having fun. I was a prototypically selfish, narcissistic young man.

But when I found tent-city, sin suddenly became a big deal. Its existence invaded my sense of self-worth and I warred against its influence in my life. At times I fought by digging my heels in and gutting out a resistance to the temptations. At other times I tried engaging an "accountability group". When my efforts failed I'd become spiritually dejected and isolative and wallow in self-abasing depression. No matter how hard I tried, I just couldn't seem to deny the urgent temptation to behave poorly.

When I reached the mountain (point A), the power encounter gave me more fire in the belly but I had no lasting authority over sin itself. I tried all the same tactics again - resistance to it, accountability group to manage it, or whatever - thinking there might be a different result since I was abiding in the mountain, but I found that there wasn't. I'd not been given the authority to abolish it in any consistent measure. Still broken, isolative and depressed, the prospect of a free and open and transparent relationship with Christ seemed like a mirage.

Then at some point the truth about sin was illuminated by new eyes.

I'd always tried to manage the behavior. That's what everybody in the pink church told me to do. But the behavior can only be stifled; it can never be abolished. When corrupted by the clown's deceit, stifling sin is never enough because only through eradication can I step boldly into the presence of a perfect God. Sin management therefore is the result of a "works-based" approach to intimacy with Christ.

In my newfound revelation, I realized that sin only holds lasting effect if I orient myself with a lie. Conversely, if I orient myself with truth, sin is blotted out of my history as though it never even occurred. On the basis of this revelation, my focus went from sin management to *heart management on the heels of sinful behavior.*

When I choose to partner with the lie that says my bad behavior has rendered me unlovable and untouchable by God, then like Romans says, *"The wages of sin is death…"* This is because my alignment with the lie effectively devalues His sacrifice and elevates me to the position of God. No longer is my salvation predicated on a free gift that I do not deserve, but by my isolative actions I'm saying that my salvation is predicated on my own ability to enter into the glory of God without His help. Impossible.

Truth about sin is exemplified by the full verse in Romans 6:23: *"For the wages of sin is death,* **but the free gift of God is eternal life in Christ Jesus our Lord."**

If on the heels of poor behavior I choose to partner with the truth that Christ came and died for sinners, and rather than isolate I run into the outstretched arms of a loving Savior, confess my bad behavior and ask His forgiveness, then the sin is blotted out from the annals of history and is as though it never happened. In this case, sin has no lasting hold on my life and I am once again the humble recipient of the free gift of grace. By partnering with truth in the moments after falling to temptation, I reestablish my true identity in Him and thereby allow his sacrifice the opportunity to fulfill its intended purpose in my life.

Adjusting my paradigm from sin management to heart management has made a world of difference in my life. It's allowed Jesus and me to live according to the roles defined by His sacrifice. He died for me, and that makes Him God. By humbly receiving his forgiveness in the moments after my sinful behavior, He gets to be God and I get to be saved all over again. But when I try and manage my own sin and isolate because of my failures, I nullify His ability to be God and nullify my own ability to be saved.

Those who abide in the clown's entanglement might listen to the whispers of deceit and accuse me, saying, "But Nate, by this rationale you are giving yourself a license to look at porn."

Or they'll accuse, "If that's the case, why don't you go murder somebody... It's not really sin if you repent, right?"

Lunacy. The accusation is categorically false, and nothing could be further from the truth. It is precisely this new perspective that furthers my drive to avoid sinful behavior.

I've come to love and cherish my true identity in Christ. I love it so much that it pains me deeply when I do things that are out of *that* character. I'm not pained by guilt or shame, I'm pained by the reality that sinful indulgence is behavior unbecoming to a citizen of the kingdom of God. I'm pained by the fact that even after all I've seen and all He's done, my broken and fallen nature still gets the better of me. I hate sin, more now than ever before not because I feel guilty about it. I hate it because I hate the way it pushes me toward isolation from the One I love.

When I was pink, I repented halfheartedly because I knew I would continue to sin. The function of repentance became like an incantation; like a formula. It was impersonal and totally ineffective. But as a mountain dweller, I repent fervently because I understand the magnitude of His sacrifice in a way that I never did before. Repentance has since taken on a whole new meaning. Ritualistic, half-hearted repentance is an action that springs out of guilt, whereas true repentance is an action that springs out of conviction, and by acting out of conviction I've seen victory over indulgence in my life.

So if I fall victim to temptation and behave in a sinful manner, and allow that action to isolate and distance me from the heart of God, then I sin, and death overtakes me as a result. But if I indulge sinful temptation and behave poorly, but humbly choose repentance and accept forgiveness through grace, that sin has indeed been forgiven and abolished from my record. In effect, it *never* happened. So then, sin's lasting spiritual effect can never be defined in the temptation or behavior that follows, it can only be defined by partnership, which is a function of my responsibility and self-determination in truth.

It's important to remember that sinful behavior constitutes a spiritual wrong first, temporal hardship second. Sin was never defined by our sense of morality. Sin was defined for us by God's perfect sense of justice. On earth, sinful behavior is par-living and frequently celebrated. In the spiritual war however, the clown tempts us to sin for only one purpose, and that is to separate us from the heart of God and debunk our sense of identity in Him. In this way, all sinful behavior is equal in the eyes of God because all sin seeks to effectuate the same outcome. This is also why the gift of salvation is equally accessible, whether I have committed a premeditated homicide, or whether I lash out at my kids.

Psalm 119: 25-29 says, *"I am laid low in the dust; preserve my life according to your word. I recounted my ways and you answered me; teach me your decrees. Let me understand the teaching of your precepts; then I will meditate on your wonders. My soul is weary with sorrow; strengthen me according to your word. Keep me from deceitful ways; be gracious to me through your law."*

The psalmist is expressing the heart of the true mountain dweller in our modern age. The pink church tries to get people to resist sinful indulgence on a moral precept, "because it's bad." The mountain dweller resists sinful behavior because it seeks to rob us of our intimacy. By the pink perspective, the resisting of sinful behavior is an act of sacrifice, but by the mountain perspective resisting it is an act of conviction.

Proverbs 28:13 says, *"He who conceals his sins does not prosper, but whoever confesses and renounces them finds mercy."*

That verse is self-explanatory, and supports exactly what I'm saying.

Colossians 3:5-6 says, *"Put to death, therefore, whatever belongs to your earthly nature: sexual immorality, impurity, lust, evil desires and greed, which is idolatry. Because of these, the wrath of God is coming."*

The perspective that I espouse in this chapter does not contradict the Word, for the Word implores us to put to death whatever belongs to our earthly nature and I could not agree more. The perspective that I espouse is merely a fundamental truth about the lasting spiritual ramifications of sin, as something that's predicated on our posture before Christ.

The pink church often claims victory in "healthy and appropriate sin management techniques". Good for them. But mountain dwellers claim victory in a promise; namely, that Christ will fulfill the good work He began in our lives as we submit to our true identity in Him, and live according to it.

The fact is I can't escape sin with power beholden to my will. Only He can nullify its effects with His gift of love, which I must choose to accept.

If you want to experience some victory in the war against sinful indulgence, dump your accountability group. Accountability groups are stupid because nobody is ever fully honest. Walk away from your presumption of tough-guy resistance; you can't fight a spiritual battle with mortal weaponry. Stop looking at the action as though it contains a mandatory minimum sentence, and try this new perspective on for size. The awesome byproduct of a sin-paradigm rooted in truth is that your indulgence will dissipate relative to His changing work in your life. Will we ever live sin-free? Nope, but guilt-free and firmly rooted in your right identity before Christ ain't too bad...

From the clown's perspective, he tempts us to sin because he is seeking to steal away intimacy with Christ. If we are ashamed, guilty by admission, and choose to isolate from God because we feel so terrible about what we just did, he won. That's why he tempts. It's not about getting you to malign somebody's character; it never was. The fact that sin sometimes carries an earthly consequence is just icing on the devil's cake.

But consider what happens if, on the heels of poor behavior you jumped into your Father's lap instead? What if, instead of concealing your dirty little secret and locking it in the basement, you confessed it to Jesus and let Him comfort you? What if, instead of adopting the identity of "worthless whore", you told Him that the behavior was unbecoming of someone whose identity is firmly rooted in Christ, apologize, and receive forgiveness?

I'll tell you what happens to the clown; he stops tempting

you in that way. Your new response represents a colossal backfire. You've rendered him 100% impotent on the battlefield of spiritual mind-games and trickery by your newfound spiritual jujitsu! Congratulations, you've just become a Jedi.

Do you feel like taking back a little ground? You want to push back on this onslaught of temptation? Adopt a change in your sin paradigm; it will do wonders.

Firm identity is the essence of spiritual warfare 101. You take the clown's intended purpose and turn it against him by identifying *you* the way Christ does. Even when circumstances seem to support the clown's accusations, align with truth. Truth doesn't change in circumstance. Truth doesn't change in behavior. Truth doesn't change because the clown concocts a pithy accusation.

Truth is that you are beautiful enough to die for.

If you don't subscribe to an identity that is rooted in how Christ sees you, you can't win a street fight with the clown. He'll always knock you out. Identity is really fundamental. It is so fundamental, in fact, that the opposite is true as well. The clown cannot beat you in a street fight if you're fighting atop the foundation of true kingdom identity.

Intellectually understanding your identity is the easy part, believing it and behaving according to it is the part that takes practice. Your identity is further solidified with every challenge you encounter and overcome in the mountain. Whether you are clearing carnage from the inside, clearing carnage from the home front, or learning to navigate as a Spirit-filled-individual in a corrupt IDP camp, each time you behave out of your kingdom identity it becomes a stronger part of who you are. The stronger your identity takes hold, the bigger your stature in the kingdom.

The street fight with the clown starts in your mind when you are coaxed into a strange world governed by powers and principalities. Sinful temptations originate in that world. Sinful indulgence often plays out in our physical realm. Then after the indulgence, we're back to the world of principalities to receive judgment or absolution for our wrongs. All the while the pink Christian engages this two-thirds-spiritual/one-third-physical engagement as a fully physical issue.

To be effective at taking back ground we must learn to fight in a world that is not our own. To do that effectively we must be willing to put on our true kingdom identity. Your identity is your armor. No man ever lasted very long in space without a spacesuit. Getting in a street fight with the clown is no different.

Chapter 15 – The Mansion

The next two chapters are heavy on stories from my life where the clown's attack went from psychological mind games to tangible hardships. The best way I know how to articulate God's purposes in these situations is to depict them in the first person, but these are just examples of what we all experience.

In the summer of 2012 I resigned from a CEO position amid a swirl of controversy involving one of the employees. The employee had been accused of sexual misconduct. As is often the case with leaders, much of the criticism pertaining to agency accountability was left at my doorstep. Fair enough. As the leader, accountability was ultimately my responsibility.

I'd been through these types of controversies in the past and had always worked hard to learn something and better the agency as a result. But contrary to the past, this incident had the clown's fingerprints all over it. This incident took on a life of its own.

Irrational anger and vitriol erupted like a volcano. Due to media intrigue, it quickly became a public spectacle. I was threatened, my family was harassed, and my character was maligned in online public forums. Former employees - years removed from the agency - called news outlets and made up stories about me and the company which added further fuel to a fire that quickly spun out of control. The whole experience was surreal. I'd never been through such a public slander-fest.

I vacationed in Orlando with my family and received daily calls from reporters fervently begging to speak with me. One reporter even called my wife. I wonder if they actually expected me to give them a comment on being called an embezzler, money launder, the leader of a Mafioso drug ring, or pimp of an underage brothel?

I was hurt by the accusations and confused about the Lord's purposes in that season. Desiring to distance myself from the madness, I worked really hard to find a new job. I was ready to do anything, and willing to move anywhere. I desperately wanted to get away from the swirl of hate. But nothing ever panned out.

Through this experience I fell into one of those deep troughs of despair in the mountain, and became angry with the Lord. I didn't understand why he was letting me and my family suffer. I didn't understand why He let the clown talk so many

"Christians" into such vile and hateful behaviors. I told the Lord, "I don't mind suffering if there's a point to it, but this just seems so pointless…"

I was in that negative headspace for some time, then, in the winter 2012 my perspective suddenly changed. The Lord gave me a vision, and in it I saw this beautiful mansion on the side of a mountain. It looked out over a city. There was a large circular upstairs patio that supplied amazing city views. The place was magnificent, like something out of Architectural Digest.

In the vision I also had a chance to walk through the city. It was loud, smelly, and extremely corrupt. There was a constant echo of sirens, as if humming the melody of a city under siege. There was a dark cloud, like smog, but even darker than that. It reeked like oil and rot.

The house in my vision was up high enough that it looked down on the cloud of smog hanging above the city. The air was sweet and crisp on the balcony, and the sounds of the city's chaos were far away and far removed. The sky was lit up with white, diamond-like stars and a crescent moon. Everything was quiet. Everything was peaceful.

In my vision I realized that I was standing in a home that Christ had built for me specifically. I walked inside and went into the dining room, and there was a picturesque Thanksgiving feast on the table, complete with turkey, ham, all the fixings and many bottles of wine. I had some friends and family with me; everyone was jovial. The kids were cute, dressed in button-ups and sweaters and on their best behavior. Oddly, I even saw myself sitting at the table and carrying on with the others. I looked happy.

My spirit then left the dining room and proceeded to a different area of the mansion. I moved through the hallways as if I knew the home well. Eventually I entered what was clearly my office. It was small and simple. There was a computer and a desk, and a small wet bar. There were two leather wingback chairs against the far wall, a few bookshelves, and a few pictures scattered about. The room was illuminated by the soft yellow glow of an overhanging light.

Looking around the room, I was perplexed as to why the vision had brought me here. Then all of a sudden it dawned on me. This was the room from which I was supposed to work.

In the midst of despair, I found energy and a sense of hope as a result of seeing that vision. The size of the mansion was irrelevant, but the people in it and the fact that it housed a quiet study were both important to me.

The Lord gave me the following interpretation.

The home He built for me is peaceful. It's not stuck in the middle of the city that decays from the inside out; rather, it's up high on a mountain. The home is close enough to the city, but far enough away. There is a part of me that lives in the city that decays, but there's also a part of me that is immortal, separate from the ruin of life on earth.

Christ showed me that my eternal dwelling place is ready for habitation immediately. Not when I die, but now. He told me that on the day He rose from the dead, He conquered death and established His new Kingdom on earth. He said that the opportunity to abide in the spiritual dwelling freely exists, and it has everything to do with my choice to move in.

As this revelation solidified, the trough of despair evaporated around me, as if it was a figment of my imagination. Once again, He raised me up to that beautiful plateau full of life. I immediately felt better, and I realized that regardless of the size of the attack, or the nature of the attack, I always retain the ability to abide in Christ Jesus. In Him I always retain the ability to enjoy peace. But the message in the vision went deeper than that.

For months I had been struggling with the concepts of provision and livelihood. Having moved up the chain of command in my previous company, I was used to being valued relative to the efforts I put forth in my work. But after resigning, my income miraculously stayed the same. Where it took 60 to 80 work hours per week as a CEO, I was suddenly working much less yet still being compensated quite well.

I *hated* getting paid well for not stressing out, not problem solving, and not being maligned and harassed in the media. In other words, I had grown addicted to justifying my salary (worth) on the basis of life's stress and turmoil. It was almost a Buddhist way of looking at life. "Justice" was that I got paid well because I had to deal with such a barrage of personal attack.

But in the vision Christ affirmed to me that my production had nothing to do with the size of the mansion He'd built for me. He affirmed that my production had nothing to do with the elaborate feast He'd provided for my friends and family. He affirmed that my production had nothing to do with how *He* valued me. It was a hard pill for me to swallow but once I did, I found that in my spirit I was suddenly able to escape the chaos of the earth and enjoy my mansion whenever I wanted.

Like others, I used to buy lottery tickets. I don't anymore. Like others, I never missed an opportunity to pull the lever of a mega millions machine in Vegas. I don't anymore. Like others, I'd lie awake at night dreaming about what I would do with a sudden influx of wealth. I used to think about whom I'd help, what I'd buy, and the peace I'd suddenly realize. But I don't do that anymore. I haven't since my paradigm shifted.

Nowadays, anytime I want, I close my eyes and simply walk into the place in which I choose to abide; my mountain estate. I sit down at the breakfast nook, imagine myself using my cell phone to call Jesus and invite him over for coffee and a bagel.

There can be no greater dream… But more than a dream, it's a reality.

For the first time in forever I realized that I didn't want to leave Colorado. I don't particularly want to go find a new job either. I'd do it if I had to, but rather than make another assumption about God's will for my life, I took a deep breath and asked a new question, *what do you want me to do?*

"I want you to write."

I remember dropping my head when he first told me. Writing didn't make a lot of sense to me. Sure, I published a book back in 2005 but ever since that time I'd done very little writing. Ever since that time I've had very little inspiration.

"What am I supposed to write about?" I argued, "*Pathways to Abandon* was a fluke. Nobody will publish the type of stuff I'd write… Agents and publishing houses alike have already said so."

"You asked." The Lord's reply was simple. He wasn't going to get into a shouting match with the clown.

"Lord, I need a real, paying job." I try a new approach; try to reason with Him. "Writing is more of a hobby, something that's fun to do. But at some point my family is going to outgrow our little home and we have debts to pay off…"

"Yeah, yeah," the Lord says with a chuckle. He must be amused by my tenacity. "Nate, I hear you, but I want you to write. What part of this are you not understanding?"

"The part where writing pays my bills, for one," I say.

"Are your bills not currently covered?" The Lord asked.

"They are, but my income could go away at any moment…"

"That's true," the Lord mused. "Your income could go away at any moment whether you're working for yourself or whether you're working for someone else. Why is it that you believe your provision is better left to your efforts than Mine? Have you ever gone without a meal?"

I swallowed hard. He was making a little too much sense.

I decided to acquiesce. I didn't fully realize it then, but by choosing to obey I was rejecting my clown-inspired need to go and derive worth through works in the city. Writing started as an act of obedience and soon became a function of great joy. Learning to become a wordsmith, creatively constructing a point; it stimulated me in ways that I've never been stimulated before.

As my fingers began bouncing around the keyboard I found inspiration for a story, a work of fiction. My inspiration was wrapped up in the research of a guy named Zeke Wheeler, and the experience of telling that story took me into a magical and wondrous place. It took just six weeks to bang out that 160,000 word novel which I titled *Splice - The Hybrid Resurgence*. As it turns out I'm pretty good at writing. I've always known that I was decent, but I never knew how much fun it could be and never dreamt I could do it full time!

At times in my journey, I've asked the Lord what His perspective is about men, and man's responsibility to provide. The Lord corrected me sternly and said, "I have not placed a responsibility of provision on men, I've placed a responsibility of livelihood. You should always work, but your provision is a function of My promise and My responsibility."

When I finally accepted the charge to write, His position on provision and livelihood was illuminated.

The reader should understand, I'm not saying people should walk away from the workplace to develop their "passions" - as Nancy Pelosi so eloquently said - on the backs of the taxpayers. That would not be right. Due to the way in which I earn income my family has technically qualified for all sorts of welfare programs, but we've never taken the assistance. That's not what welfare is for. Just because circumstances make something available does not mean that I'd be partnering with truth by taking it. I'm not saying people should avoid taking welfare if their need is justified, but able-bodied individuals (and men in particular) should work, and do so with a right identity firmly rooted in the mountain.

We take back spiritual ground when we choose to abide in the mountain and reject the clown's assertion that our worth is measured by our production. It never was. Do we measure the worth of our children on the basis of their production? Of course not. By this rationale our children would be worthless.

If we, the broken and corrupt have the ability to love our children outside of a production paradigm, how much more does our perfect and infallible God have the ability to love us? Production-centered value can be a difficult thing to identify, but I've come up with a few indicators.

Do you struggle to ask for help? Are your revelatory experiences, proximity to Christ, or standing in the church a thing of personal pride? Do you get excited when a well-known person or "public figure" notices you? Do you minimize your sin life when talking to trustworthy others? Does your cell phone have permission to interrupt face-to-face conversations? When people ask how you're doing, does your go-to answer have something to do with how busy you are?

There are a ton of other indicators, but you get the point. It's impossible to live in an eternal realm when we are chained to a temporal one. It's impossible to fully experience freedom and habitation in our kingdom dwelling place if we are addicted to our habitation on earth. In order to get to the mountain, you have to leave the IDP camp behind.

The astute reader understands that by asking God to remove pride and a production-centered value system, you're essentially asking for *death to self*. Death to self is as violent and painful as it sounds. I prayed for death to self regularly, and then I entered into that season in 2012 where I and my family came under vicious assault. In that hour I cried out to the Lord and said, "I don't mind suffering if there is a point, but there is no point to this…"

Of course there was a point; He was merely answering my prayers. I was just too arrogant to see it.

Pink

Chapter 16 - When It Gets Physical

The clown's accusations rarely derail me because they hold no weight of authority against my true identity in Christ. They are just the misguided musings of a defeated foe. When psychological warfare becomes ineffective, he often petitions God for permission to up the ante. Sometimes, God gives him the green light. We see evidence of this in Scripture, not just in the Book of Job, but in the way the Apostles and Prophets were often hunted and murdered for simply obeying the will of the Lord.

On March 2, 2014 the clown's attack became physical for me in a profound way. I had just finished a depressing cigar with a few friends after the Seattle Seahawks put a hellacious curb-stomp to the neck of the Denver Broncos in the Super Bowl. Bummed out about the game, I decided to walk home. I left my friend's house around 9 PM.

I walk a lot because it's cathartic for me to spend quiet time in prayer and introspection. When I walk I talk to Him like a friend, and He talks to me that way too. The air was chilly but the night was peaceful and uneventful until I was a half mile from my friend's house. Then, I was suddenly attacked by two pit bulls.

Like ghost dogs they emerged from a dark alley, growling. Startled, I changed direction and headed to the other side of the street but they came up to me and postured. I said something like *stop, go away,* and that's when the one nearest to my left side lunged. He sunk his jaw into my left forearm and began flailing around as if trying to rip my arm off.

Terrified, I screamed as the other dog circled around to my rear. I applied pressure into the jowl of the first dog and he released his grip. As the second dog crept in tight, I swung a foot in his direction and he backed up. For five minutes those dog circled around, menacingly taunting. Slowly I was able to retreat from their block and eventually they let me go.

Heart pounding I took a long detour to avoid their patrol zone. My arm throbbed like crazy and I wanted to get a look at the damage but I was wearing multiple layers including a thick parka, so I decided to continue walking to the nearest gas station. It was about a mile and a half away.

When I reached the gas station I took my coat off and gingerly pulled up the sleeve of my hoodie. The dog had done quite a number on my left forearm. Crushed but not lacerated, it had already started turning many shades of black and blue. I snapped a picture and sent it via text message to a few buddies. I was shocked by the horrible ordeal but made a joke about getting jumped by two pit bulls in the text. I didn't bother to watch as their replies began flooding into my phone.

Though it throbbed, I knew there was nothing I could do at that hour so I decided to go home and sleep it off. I'd get the wound looked at in the morning. I put all the clothing back on and left the 7-Eleven at around 10:15 PM. I was certain that my excitement was over… Boy, was I wrong.

As I left the 7-Eleven there were two cars parked at the curb. One was colored in a light paint, the other was dark - maybe black or dark blue - and I remember a fleeting moment where something deep inside me warned of danger. A momentary glance at the dark vehicle revealed the silhouette of somebody sitting in the driver spot, but I recall nothing else. Pushing the feeling aside I turned north and walked to the edge of the 7-Eleven, hit the sidewalk and headed east toward the downtown corridor. I still had four miles to walk so my pace was brisk.

About two minutes later I was standing at an intersection

waiting for the light to turn when a loud *bang* rang out and immediately I felt as though my *left arm* - yes, the exact same arm that had been bitten by the dog - had been blown off my shoulder. The pain is hard to describe. I've told friends that it felt like somebody dunked my arm into a vat of acid, then ran an electrical current through it, and then lit the whole thing on fire. It was an awful zinging, buzzing sort of pain that entirely eclipsed the throb from the dog bite.

At the initial moment of pain I twirled around clockwise and staggered. My hand had bunched itself into a contorted fist and I could not move my fingers. Heart racing, I looked at the intersection and in the passenger seat of the light-colored vehicle was a young woman, her eyes wide as saucers, staring at me. No doubt she was wondering what happened. I needed help and thought about asking her to help me, but the light changed and she drove away. Somewhere in my subconscious I have a faint memory of a separate set of taillights attached to a dark-colored vehicle speeding away.

I turned to go back to the 7-Eleven. Something was really wrong, the pain in my arm was unlike anything I'd ever felt. I was strangely disoriented. Halfway to the 7-Eleven I stopped, and decided I did not want to go back there. There was a Denny's next to me, but I'd passed the front door so I doubled back and gingerly walked in.

I did not know what had happened, so when the waitress asked what she could do to help I simply said, "Help me get my jacket off."

She assisted, and as my left jacket sleeve pitched forward a river of blood flowed out of it. She gasped and dropped the jacket, went straight to the register, picked up the phone and dialed 911.

I sat on the edge of a booth and fumbled through my jacket pockets looking for my phone. I found it and it beeped, signifying low battery. I hit the text message icon and blindly tapped one of the top threads, hoping my friends had not gone to bed yet. The last question one of them asked was, *do you need help?*

As the first of the police officers arrived I hastily typed, "yes, ambulances coming, at Denny's."

Next I was surrounded by emergency medical personnel and a few police officers. They took my hoodie off and immediately diagnosed that I'd been shot. The bullet entered my forearm and blasted out the other side, less than an inch from where the dog bit me 45 minutes prior. Predictably the cops had a hard time believing my story at first, but after they had an opportunity to construct the timeline using the various text messages I sent, they realized I was telling the truth. That night, as I was rolled out of Denny's on a stretcher there were a couple dozen officers combing the area, looking for evidence of an attempted homicide.

I wasn't caught between gang crossfire; in fact I was the only pedestrian on the road. Whoever did this aimed at me and made a conscious decision to shoot. Whoever did this was trying to kill me. It actually took days for this realization to settle in.

In the weeks following, my mind was a mess. I went through what I assume is a typical emotional roller coaster, starting with hurt and confusion. The *why me?* season. That led to a period of *fear*, during which time I had a hard time going outside at night. Irrationally, I felt like somebody was always around the next bend, ready and willing to finish the failed attempt. Fear for me was the toughest season.

Then at some point I left fear and fell into *anger*, and envisioned myself finding the perpetrator and ending his miserable life in a personal way. Anger still wells up in me from time to time, but that too has basically passed. As the roller coaster screeched to a halt at the docking station, I came into the season I find myself in now, best described by the simple word *peace*.

A pastor friend of mine told me that in Scripture, the left arm or hand signify intimacy. The bizarre nature of this attack was punctuated by the fact that both the dog and the bullet found their way to my left arm. Intimacy with Christ is what has given me the authority to write this book, and intimacy with Christ has been the foundation of my pursuit and understanding since arriving at point A of the journey. Intimacy is the whole game, and the clown will go to great lengths to hijack it.

Some - to include the clown - have since asked, "So where was God when He let you get shot?"

He was right there, making sure the bullet didn't hit an artery or major organ. He was right there, making sure that the shooter failed to get off a second round. He was right there, making sure that this incident took place at a time when I was alone, away from my wife and children.

With respect to my standpoint on the left-hand of

intimacy, others have asked, "So why did God let the enemy take a swipe at your intimacy?"

Because by allowing my confidence to be shook, it's also been healed and rebuilt anew. It's stronger now; it's more resilient. As wind strengthens the root structures of trees, so too are we strengthened by the conflicts of attack. By allowing me an opportunity to experience an attack such as this, the attacks that come as a result of challenging the pink church will be more tolerable. He didn't have to let me survive that attack, but since he did I'm of the opinion that I've got nothing to lose now, and confidence abounds.

The clown's intention was not just to rattle my faith and steal away my intimacy. It was also meant to inhibit what the Lord has called me to do in this season of my life, which is writing. I was only two chapters into this book when I got shot, and even as I dictate this sentence, I still lack the use of my left hand. It's made the process harder, slower. But difficulty aside, the Lord truly usurped the enemy's intention by giving me a profound joy in this journey. Sure, it's slower and more difficult to write a book with cumbersome dictation software, but it's still coming. Soon it will be finished.

Sometimes, the attack will get physical. We experience the

physical attack when bad things happen to good people, or loved ones suddenly die, or random illness overtakes a healthy body. I am certainly not the only one who has ever undergone such an assault; indeed, the vast majority of us have.

When the attack gets physical, the clown's intention is to disgrace our image of a loving God. This is why agnostics all over the planet will say that they can't get behind the idea of a "loving God" because of all the hurt and pain and evil in the world. You've heard it before, and maybe even said it yourself, "If God is so good, why does He let so many bad things happen to good people?"

The clown's playbook is simple and unoriginal. Whether he's attacking with mind games and trickery, or whether he gets permission to shoot you in cold blood, the entire purpose of his engagement is to convince you that God is bad. But truth is, bad things happen because the clown is effectuating them at will within the parameters of his permission within a fallen Earth.

Rather than look at it as God effectuating bad things, understand that good things would not ever happen without God. God is just in permitting the evil; what He doesn't have to do (but does anyway) is perfect the evil and make good come out of it.

Whether dealing with psych games or physical assaults, the one who abides in the mountain maintains a perspective of truth, and holds fast to the promises Jesus made. The clown's argument is categorically false, but he's masterful at using challenging circumstances to confound the spiritually lazy.

Lazy is not me, by evidence of my spiritual state after being shot, and by evidence of my willingness to write this book and put it out as is. I don't blame God when mortality overtakes the mortal. I don't blame God when our humanism justifies evil. I don't blame God when the enemy behaves out of his design, and I certainly don't blame God because I'm too damn lazy to come up with a better explanation for why evil exists in the world.

In the analogy of my journey through the mountain, this shooting incident has only served to propel me up yet another cliff. I'd be stuck in the trough of despair if I'd listened to the clown, but I didn't. Well, I might have in the beginning, but I've since turned away from that.

I fully acknowledge the sovereignty of God in this event and in doing so, He's raised me up yet again. I've temporarily lost the use of my left hand for the purposes of typing on the computer, but I've received so much more in return. My heart is fuller than it ever has been in my life. I'm more energized, confident, and fearless than before. Newfound, uncommon confidence is what enables me to write this book with open transparency, without a smidgen of concern for how you ultimately receive it. If my articulation and delivery work well for you, praise God. If it doesn't, fine. Maybe someday I'll get a second chance to present it.

Had it not been for the clown's failed attempts in my life, I could never have experienced the power of redemption, the sweet kiss of intimacy, or the assurance that comes through radical abandonment. I could not have loved, for there would be nothing on which to hang my gratitude. No standard of measure by which to comprehend a completely foreign life in Christ. Pain and struggle propel me into the mountain; excess and luxury tell me that I don't need a Savior.

Allowing evil to exist and bad things to happen is an act of mercy. Pink Christians could never understand this because they are hell-bent on finding filet mignon in the desert, joy in the brothels of Tijuana, security in knowledge, health through medicine, and life on earth.

This book isn't for everybody. Analogies make no sense to the deaf and blind. That's why Christ used them back in His time, and that's why He still uses them today through dudes He knows and trusts.

When the attack gets physical, there is no separate application for how to deal with the scheming lies of the clown. Whether the attack is physical or psychological, our response must remain firmly rooted in the values we know to be true. As we align ourselves to truth we can be confident that He will never miss an opportunity to raise us up to a higher place in Him.

Chapter 17 – Ripped off the Hooks

Most of this section has been about the very personal attack the clown wages on individuals, and speaks to how the willing might exact a spiritual reversal in their lives. Chapter 18 and 19 are different. This next section is based in prophetic insights about what's coming. Soon, the sheep will be ripped off the clown's rusty hooks and when she does, the IDP camp will start crumbling.

For the sake of imagery, agree with me that the IDP camp is a huge, sprawling metropolis. It's a city that houses roughly 2.18 billion people. Anyone who has ever declared faith in Christ Jesus has been given entry. There is no litmus test at the gate, no customs or border enforcement to speak of. Simply attest to your tentative faith in Christ and you will be given a beautiful single-wide, two-ply, prefabricated tent. Welcome to the place the clown wants you to believe is the promised land.

The camp has been segregated into hundreds of thousands of regions. Each region has its own standards, expectations, and core beliefs. There are Orthodox regions and many subsets. There are evangelical regions and many denominations. Each one of these regions has a central Main Street running through the middle of it, and that's where the people gather to worship. It's also where they buy and sell, and it's where the clown keeps a watchful eye over the happenings.

Anybody is allowed to redefine the districts. In fact, it's encouraged. When anger and disillusionment abound, the clown expects young new leaders to emerge and petition for regional autonomy. In this way truth is no longer a pure white, but has become many shades of pink. Pure white is a powerful disruptor, a catalyst to civil unrest. By splicing truth with as many additives as possible, the sociopolitical structures of the IDP camp remain stable.

There are three basic demographics in this camp. The first demographic constitutes the huge majority. They live in prefabricated tents and hang around with others in their region. Most of these folks are pretty simple. Some of them volunteer on their neighborhood's Main Street, but most of them leave the camp when they go to work every morning, and return in the afternoon once their work day concludes. These guys freely cross both sides of the camp's barrier, and are generally easy-going about their faith.

They like exploring the intricacies of doctrine, but they have never been convinced of the need to get hard-core and delve into the mountain. It's not to say that they wouldn't, it's just not something they've ever been told is necessary. Intellectually, they understand that the IDP camp is huge, but they've never seen the other regions so their understanding is limited by their narrow base of experience.

The second demographic is remarkably large, and consists of the men and women who govern each Main Street. Their association to Main Street has given them certain perks, not the least of which is an identity as a "Christian somebody". Like the first demographic, many of these inhabitants are well-intentioned and genuine, and others aren't.

These are the men and women who run all sorts of ministries: Christian media outlets, Christian colleges, Christian schools, Christian outreach programs and huge Christian conferences. This demographic is not defined by whether or not they genuinely love; it's defined by their reliance on a robust Christian-centered marketplace and economy.

Within the second demographic you have people classified as leaders, teachers, pastors, prophets, evangelists, apostles, bankers, insurance agents, attorneys, gift shop owners and Christian booksellers. These are the people who rely on the Christian dollar for their livelihood. Christian authors, Christian moviemakers, missionaries, ministry builders, and all sorts of other folks fall into this category as well.

Association with the second demographic certainly does not define the individual as a good or bad person. It's just a designation that is separate from those of the first, who, though they may take their faith seriously choose to not identify as a Christian leader or businessperson.

Finally there is a third demographic, by far the smallest group. They are represented by people from both the first and second demographic. They are the ones who sneak away from the camp at night and spend serious time in the mountain. They come from all walks of life. Some of them are entrenched in the *industry* while others are outside of it. Some of them have a deep understanding of Christian dogma, some don't. Some of them have been convinced about Christ for decades, others were convinced only days ago. What this demographic shares is a pursuit, a courageous pursuit of intimacy that goes far beyond the norm seen within the greater encampment.

The third demographic is becoming the beast. The third demographic is being turned into the beast, almost outside of their will. The beastly form manifests as their eyes open and they begin to perceive the atrocities commonplace within the Christian IDP camp. As the third demographic grows intimate with Christ, they begin to share in His suffering. They stop seeing the atrocities commonplace on Main Street as the failed attempts of well-meaning leaders; they begin to see literal treaties and alliances between various leaders and the clown. The third demographic is beginning to emerge, but is not a vocal minority yet. These folks have not found their voice.

When the third demographic finds their voice, a Civil War will break out between those who remain in the second and those who have become part of the third. The Civil War will cause the IDP camp to empty, and every inhabitant will be forced to choose a new dwelling place. Those who choose the world will suddenly be called "friend" by the titans of popular culture. The clown will reward them for their choice to relocate in the world by establishing big new gaudy church buildings, prominent platforms, and a doubled down message. Those who refuse the world will be forced to take refuge in the mountain and relocate there.

The emptying of the IDP camp will not signify the end of the war, but the beginning. When this happens, the mountain people will be called heretics and radicals, racists and bigots, and *dangerous*. They will be ostracized by the Christian majority who boldly assert that theirs is true Christianity - a religion of peace. Then the mountain dwellers will be publicly scorned, denigrated, and slandered in every way imaginable.

As the number of mountain dwellers increases, so shall the ferocity of the clown. As the war progresses the clown will petition for permission to bring a greater measure of attack against those who have decided to put their trust in Christ *alone*. Even at the expense of those who he has already enslaved, the clown will see to it that the global economy first jitters, then crashes to the ground. He'll do this because he knows that above all else, humanity is addicted to the false sense of security they feel in money.

When this happens, those who dwell in the mountain will be cut off from the marketplace. It will become difficult to buy and sell goods, and the clown will use economy as a way to starve them of hope. But it will not work because like in the days of old, Christ will rain manna down from heaven and uphold His promise of provision. Within the mountain there will be resources, and people will come together and provide for one another. The clown's economic efforts will thus fail.

Next, the clown will convince the secular governments of the world that mountain dwellers pose an imminent and serious risk to their governance. They will believe him when he calls us "enemy combatants" and "terrorists". New laws will come into effect that designate mountain dwellers as criminals, and this is when the attack will go physical on a global scale.

Some will be imprisoned and others will be killed, and all the while hundreds of thousands will join us in the mountain, fully convinced that their trust is well-placed in Christ. In that hour, there will be a population explosion in the mountain because of the hopelessness and distress that will flow through the cities of the world. In the mountain there will be lasting peace and joy amidst grief and sorrow. In the world there will only be sorrow.

These things, details notwithstanding, must all come to pass because they've been prophesied.

When regular men and women living in the IDP camp begin rejecting the status quo by pursuing individual relationships with Christ, the structural principles that hold the IDP camp together will begin to wobble. As more of us experience the mountain, more pressure will be applied to those structures, and eventually the whole thing will come crashing down. This is in effect, the pink sheep getting ripped off the clown's meat hooks.

Chapter 18 – The Voice of the Beast

Many within the second demographic of the IDP camp have a clear and precise understanding of their identity in Christ as well as their destiny on earth. The Lord has shown them that they are to be (and maybe already behave as) authentic Pastors, Teachers, Evangelists, Prophets, Apostles, or other servants of the faith.

Likewise, there are many leaders in the camp who have been convinced by the clown that their role designation is to prop up falsities. In this metropolis, authentic leaders and wolves live in close proximity to one another and are sometimes hard to distinguish. Not because they execute their responsibilities the same, but because the inhabitants of the encampment lack the sagacity to know the difference between friend and foe.

All of us are spiritual beings, and all of us possess a special grace that enables clear communication with and through the Holy Spirit. The deep mysteries of faith are therefore uniquely illuminated as we individually choose to navigate the mountain's highlands and lowlands, byways and highways, peaks and valleys. Because we are all created spiritual, we all partake in the gifts of the Spirit. We prophesy, we speak in tongues, we see the lame walk and the mute speak. We all experience the supernatural side of life because of how we were created. The supernatural stuff is rare in the IDP camp, but once you enter the mountain it becomes commonplace.

Well beyond the uniformity of access, we all have the opportunity to exercise specific spiritual gifts in very specific ways in life. Moses, David, Abraham, Peter, John, Esther, Mary and Elijah are examples of men and women whom God selected to be specialized ambassadors of His will in their generation. But it goes further than that. Pharaoh, Jezebel, Nebuchadnezzar, Judas, Caiaphas and Hitler are examples of exactly the same thing, people who were divinely selected to fulfill certain other roles in their generation.

From a dogmatic perspective, do I believe that these people were walking corpses from the moment they were born? Did they not have a chance to fulfill a positive purpose in their life? Honestly, I'm not sure. At some level they had to have exercised the same free-will we all do, but I think the Lord used them nevertheless to fulfill certain requirements of His greater purpose.

Point is, from the beginning of recorded history God has divinely selected and used individuals to fulfill certain roles, and our generation is no different. Though we all share the ability and grace to experience the gifts of the Spirit, the Lord is calling *individuals* to fulfill specific functions.

The beast has not yet found its voice, but some have begun calling attention to certain outrages in the streets and alleys of tent-city. Though it has not constituted a major jolt, the rage is beginning to build. So far, the third demographic is only known by its inner grumble, a growing discontent with the status quo. But all that is going to change when authentic leaders begin to arise.

Teachers, Pastors, and Evangelists must continue working out of the grace that the Lord has given them. Their role is to interpret, shepherd and share respectively, and some are doing a fine job. But when we distill the pink goo of Christian faith down to its fundamental elements, we find that it has been allowed to thrive because of the abject failure on the part of authentic Prophets and Apostles. When will the Apostles start openly challenging the abomination that is pink Christianity? When will authentic Prophets start delivering truth-filled uncut messages?

The sagacious are not so quick to proclaim themselves an Apostle or a Prophet! The pink church has thrived on our watch. Where Teachers, Pastors, and Evangelists are called to interpret, shepherd, and share, Apostles and Prophets are called to lead with courage and prophesy with sagacity.

Within the pink church the role of the Prophet has been vilified, misunderstood, and excommunicated. The clown doesn't want Prophets anywhere near the IDP camp because they wield an authority with the power to destroy the metropolis. Likewise, these days it seems as though everybody is an Apostle. It's the new sexy buzzword that gets tossed around so much that every pacifist milksop who's figured out how to merge his life in Christ with that of the world believes himself to be an *Apostle*. Really? If Peter and Paul were the standard-bearers, are the so-called Apostles of this generation measuring up? 2 Corinthians 12:12 tells us that we would know true Apostles by the authority they carry in wisdom and by the supernatural wonders they perform. I don't see a lot of wisdom. I don't see a lot of authority. Do you?

Likewise, authentic Prophets have historically been fiercely committed to the offensive truth. The label of *false prophet* is reckoned to soothsayers and the politically correct. If

Samuel and Elijah were the standard-bearers among our ancestors, are the Prophets of this generation coming close to measuring up?

In the book of Acts, Apostles confronted evil anytime they encountered it. It didn't matter if they were confronting a lewd spirit hovering over a group of people, or confronting it amongst themselves. They didn't end a dispute without coming to the truth of the matter in Christ, and they certainly did not "agree to disagree". Whether they were able to rectify their differences in the moment or not, their identity was one man before God and one kingdom before Christ, *united*. By submitting to Christ, differences were regularly flushed out through revelation and humility.

Authentic Apostles do not witness atrocity and turn away because of exhaustion, or because they were afraid of confrontation. Our forbearers were all massacred for choosing, with courage and sagacity, to confront the clown in their generation. The would-be Apostles and Prophets of this day are more like life-coaches, presenters of the ever evolving 12-step program on how to avoid conflict and splice the kingdom of God with the kingdom of earth.

Pink

Make no mistake; if the good news of Christ Jesus is not wildly confrontational, then the message is *pink*. Every element of authentic truth grates against the powers and principalities that govern the earth, not the least of which is the humanist spirit. Everything from His love paradigm to His righteous judgment, it all confronts the human psyche because the clown has convinced the world to view anything Christ-centric as offensive.

Christianity is not a faith of peace or compromise at all. Who told you that? Christ himself proclaims in Matthew 10, *"Do not think that I came to bring peace to earth. I have not come to bring peace, but a sword. I've come to set a man against his father, and a daughter against her mother, and a daughter-in-law against her mother-in-law…"*

Christ did not come to save jerk-offs who align themselves with the clown. He came to save His beloved who align themselves with *Him*. That's why there is a war. Everybody wants what He's offering, but nobody wants it at the expense of their love affair with the clown. People have every right to take what's freely offered, but not while keeping a *gumar* on the side.

Christ compromised nothing, and never came to make peace with the world. He came to divide the world; His people and everybody else. His beloved will either choose to abide in Him or they won't. Abiding in Christ means living in the mountain and being targeted for attack as a result. To abide outside the mountain, to include the not-fully-in and not-fully-out fence known as the IDP camp, is to live in absolute and total separation from God because it constitutes absolute and total rejection of Christ.

This idea that you can be half in and half out is categorically false. We are either fully in, or fully out.

True Apostles don't turn a blind eye to heretic messages, misinterpretations, or the "easy life" doctrine. They reject the notion that firm values could ever be used as a negotiation tool with the world. True Apostles who have come up in the mountain don't care if truth offends, because theirs is first and foremost a calling to the truth, not a calling to the insecurities of the lost. Nobody said they have to be ass-holes in the delivery of truth. Nobody said empathy was a bad thing, but true Apostles could never compromise truth. This is not something that they could endure based on what they've seen and Who they've interacted with in the mountain. Assuredly, if I call myself a Prophet but refuse to do the will of my Father, others will rise up in my place according His justice in the years to come. If you call yourself an authentic Prophet but refuse to deliver your Father's message, you will be cut down and replaced in the years to come.

Apostles are given to bring stability to chaos, correction to corrosive messaging, and counsel to the leadership established by the vertical hierarchy. They are those whom we look to *first* for guidance and firm standards. Their call is to define truth and justice, and furnish wise counsel. The pink church will cease to exist when the Apostles find their voice.

Likewise, true Prophets don't care if they get "kicked out of the church" because theirs is a message that's often better screamed from the mountain top. Since when did Prophets require that their message was liked, appreciated, and somehow accredited by the prevalent wisdom in the pink church? When did Prophets become insecure imps who needed the warm fuzzy blanket of affirmation? True Prophets know that theirs is a message that will always be rejected by the religious leaders and money launderers.

Prophets, either stand up and speak with some backbone or do yourself a huge favor and stop talking altogether. God will not take kindly to your cowardice. Your office represents the pinnacle of wisdom and courage. The office cannot be occupied without it.

If you're convinced that you are a Prophet or an Apostle and yet you lack the will or ability to confront the wrongs in and among your sphere of influence, then take a sabbatical and get right with Jesus in the mountain. Prophets and Apostles do not have the luxury of letting things go, turning a blind eye, or letting the sun set on an atrocity. Theirs is a responsibility that extends over the kingdom. It's first and foremost a responsibility to the heart of God.

Some will say, "Yes, I hear you! The injustice burns in my gut too but I don't have a platform to speak out or do anything about it…"

Au contraire, everybody has a platform in the age of the Internet; but beside the point, your call is never defined by the size of your sphere of authority. If you are just in your assessment of what's going on around you, and bring correction in the name of the Lord with courage and sagacity, you fulfill the mandate of your office whether you are speaking to one or 1 million. According to God's timing, platforms develop where willingness and authentic truth collide.

If however, you are false in your assessment of what's going on around you and attempt to bring correction in the name of the Lord, either your platform will not expand and the Lord will correct you, or your platform will expand and you will be labeled a wolf before the end comes.

Stepping into the office of the Apostolic or Prophetic *is* stepping into the lion's den, and you will be forced to face down frightening attacks and even attempts on your life. Eventually, when your role has been fulfilled, there is absolutely no reason to assume that your life will end in a way contrary to the Apostles of the first century. Espousing another point of view or doctrine with regard to this wholly unique and extremely *unsexy* call of duty in Christ, is categorically false.

The men and women of the third demographic are the beast. The beast will be made up of the divinely chosen - the Davids and Elijahs of this generation. They will all share in a call of duty that incites a terrible Civil War that shall usher in the foretold season of the great harvest.

This chapter is not written to the men and women of the first demographic. This chapter is written to the men and women who are destined to be transformed into the true and authentic leaders of this generation. The great call of our age is to rip the pink sheep off the clown's hooks and to ignite a nuclear bomb in the center of the pink church. The IDP camp must be destroyed. It's not gonna be pretty. It's gonna be messy. But if you read the words in this book and your heart rate picks up, your hands begin to perspire, and a sense of righteous anger starts crawling up your spine, be open to what the Lord may be asking you to do right now.

Chapter 19 - Birthright, Inheritance and Destiny

God honored the promises He made to the nation's father, Abraham, when He led the sons and daughters of truth out of captivity in the land of Egypt. Upon reaching the Sinai Peninsula, amid mass chaos and confusion, the Israelites pitched their tents in the dusty valley and built for themselves a graven image, a golden calf. It's a scene that is so linear and yet so profoundly cyclical.

From the rocky riverbeds of the ancient world, this epic has continued through the ages. The IDP camp is the bloodiest battlefield the world has ever known. The clown's relevance to this war is eternally tied to humanity. His attack only exists because of our design, because God saw fit to endow every man and woman with the gift of free will. The clown has no capacity to wage war directly with God on his own, for the only weapons accessible to him are the hearts and minds of people. The clown has no authority to fight God, only we do.

This is why ours is not a war of flesh and blood, but a war waged by the principalities of good and evil. Spilled blood is merely the physical manifestation. The spiritual realm does not respond to incantations about truth, only to partnerships *with* it.

We have all been gifted with free will but to millions of us it's become a curse. This is because whether we like it or not, we're all in a winner-take-all death match where only the sagaciously courageous survive. And according to the principalities that govern this war, which is frighteningly misunderstood, our lot in life is to either win or lose everything.

The pink live as though they've relinquished free will. They don't want intimacy, they want sacrifice and servitude. They don't want freedom, they want containment. They don't want a promise, they prefer rules. This isn't because they fundamentally reject intimacy; rather, it's because the clown has convinced them to never experience it. Intimacy is everything. It was everything in the Sinai Valley, it's everything today, and it is everything for the rest of time.

God created His love interest when he breathed life into the lungs of our species. We shall become the bride of the Almighty. This is no small thing, and it's what makes us different from every other creation, including the clown. A household pet is unsuitable for marriage. Angels who lack the gift of self-determination are unsuitable for marriage. Only a species with the capacity to engage his surroundings the same way God does could ever be truly suitable for intimacy.

To become the unified bride is the charge of this generation. We don't build the kingdom; we choose to abide in it. As we do so with courage and sagacity, the kingdom populates around us. Reclaiming the courage and sagacity needed to boldly approach the mountain ablaze requires intentionality. Is your heart right for the journey? Are you ready to plunge deeper than you ever thought you could?

If your answer is yes, what comes next?

First we must repent. We must repent for aligning with a nefarious foe. We must repent for our own part in furthering the apathy that has consigned so many to a life of despair and heartache. Repentance illuminates the wondrous sacrifice made by Christ Jesus, and through that revelation we become convicted to leave the IDP camp behind and embark on an extraordinary journey into the great unknown.

Then, as we enter the mountain, we know ahead of time that circumstances and feelings are apt to validate the whispers of deceit. Being forewarned, we prep ourselves to reject the lies and align with truth, even when it's difficult. In this way, brick by brick we start building a new dwelling place, one that is etched straight into the mountain granite. This is the life we choose, and we do so knowing and expecting a daily street fight with a desperate clown.

As we persevere, He conquers. As He conquers, our stature grows. As our stature grows the powder-puff attacks of yesterday go from being a debilitating crisis to a running joke. We overcome through Christ and we link arms with the fellowship of His beloved. Though your experiences will be unique, you won't be the only one in the mountain. We are all in this together.

Some time ago I saw a vision that excited me in a way that's hard to describe. It was empowering and convicting and inspiring, and it seems fit to conclude this book with it.

As the vision opened my eyes settled on a young man, a teenager. He was lying in a gooey trough of black slime in the middle of a great expanse. The land was full of sharp jagged rocks and black slime. It was gloomy and dim and the goo covering everything was the consistency of tar; sticky and rank.

Pink

The black slime appeared to have a life essence to it. It poked and prodded at the man, and I watched as he tried to scramble to his feet. He looked exhausted. Each time he tried to stand up, the slime tripped him and pulled him back under. He clutched at his midsection as though his stomach hurt, he winced with pain, and I came to understand that the black slime was literally draining the life right out of him.

He kept fighting and then I saw in the distance a being approach. He had the form of a man but was taller and with broader shoulders. He looked like a warrior. He walked toward us, his eyes bright as if illuminated by an inner glow. The slime appeared to have no effect on him. He reached down and took the teenager by the arm and helped him up. The warrior had a huge sword, and armor that glistened and shimmered; not as though it reflected light, but as though it imparted it. Near to where he stood the slime led away slinking into the distance as if trying to avoid contact with the warrior.

The teenager brushed himself off and immediately I saw his countenance lift. His facial muscles relaxed and though he looked exhausted, a fire was beginning to flicker in his eyes. The warrior then pointed in the opposite direction and there, not far away was a towering mountain. At the base of the mountain was an arched opening from which light poured into the desolate expanse. As if understanding his gesture, the teenager began limping toward it and I followed.

At the threshold of the opening I gasped, the light was so bright and the spirit was so powerful that I did not know if I could survive walking inside. One baby step at a time, I followed the teenager in and watched as he collapsed with exhaustion.

Next, I was in a brightly lit room, and it seemed as though every color of the rainbow danced in the air. There was a stretcher, and on the stretcher I saw the teenager from the great expanse. He was shirtless, and from his chest the black tar was oozing out of him, as if being drawn out through his pores. When the slime interacted with the air inside the mountain however, it evaporated like smoke. I got the sense that he was being purged of the grinding gunk that had clung to him in the great expanse.

People dressed in robes were walking to and fro, laughing and joking with one another. The room then emptied and I watched as the boy sat up.

He looked strong. Something was different about him. His jaw was firmer, his muscles were relaxed but larger, and there was a sense of authority and power in his expressions and movements.

I then heard something that drew my attention. Laughter. It was coming from an adjacent room; the sounds of camaraderie and joy. It tugged at my attention. I glanced at the teen and noticed that he too was curious.

I followed him down a short hallway and we walked into a huge dining hall. The spread was unlike anything I'd ever seen. The smells were orgasmic. Everyone appeared to be having the time of their life. Before I could take it all in, a stout fellow with a red beard and bushy eyebrows grabbed the teen by his shoulder and pulled him into a group. There was such a natural sense of belonging. In that great hall I was surrounded by people I did not know, but this was the most comfortable place I've ever been.

The vision then flashed forward; how long I could not tell. Again I stood next to the teen as a woman approached and told him that it was time for him to go to the armory.

I followed him there, and in the armory he was given a razor-sharp sword not made of steel, but of light. The steward then withdrew an enormous set of armor, sized to fit a giant.

"That's too big for me," he said, smiling. In my mind I agreed with his assessment.

"No it's not," the steward said. "Just put it on."

The teen did as instructed and to our mutual surprise, the armor fit perfectly. He put on shoulder guards, spiked forearm guards, a breastplate, leg and shin guards, and new boots. There was a cape that swung off of one shoulder, and the entire ensemble was clasped together with jewels. It wasn't until he got the armor on that I noticed a marked change in everything about him.

He no longer looked like a teenager. His face was fierce and his physique was huge. His muscles bulged and he looked invincible. I staggered back with a sense of awe when he turned toward me. He was at once the most frightening yet approachable man I'd ever seen in my life.

Next I followed him out of the mountain and into the great and desolate expanse. I could see more clearly now. Hundreds of thousands; millions and billions were writhing and thrashing in the slime, fighting for their lives. The teenager-turned-warrior stood to my left, and beyond him stood three others who were adorned in similar attire. Ambassadors of the mountain, they were full of a power not their own.

I noticed thick veins bulging in his neck, clearly marking the intensity of his demeanor. The warrior clinched his jaw. Rage was boiling over and his eyes gleamed with violence.

I wondered what was making him so mad when I looked into the expanse and saw for myself. For the first time, I saw not a horde of people getting twisted and turned by the potent attack of the slime, but my friends. My family. These were not the nameless and faceless majority, these were people I knew. They weren't supposed to be out here. They were supposed to be in the mountain! Why weren't these loved ones in the safety of the mountain?

They were gasping for air and fighting with everything they had, but many were floundering. My heart raced; I needed to try and do something but I couldn't. I was merely an observer, unable to communicate with anyone or anything in this desolate wasteland. In my spirit I cried out. I asked the Lord to intervene and the Lord answered.

Like a deep rumble from the depths of the mountain He said, "I have given you Prophets and Apostles, Teachers and Pastors and Evangelists. Let them arise in this generation!"

As those words rumbled into the distance, the Warriors drew their swords and ran headfirst into the carnage. True ambassadors of the kingdom of God had been dispatched. They tore through the slime with swords blazing and cut the bonds and chains that held the people captive. The people who were cut free started running. Hundreds of thousands began piling into the mountain...

The day I saw that vision was the day I decided there was no turning back from the life I had chosen. Not for me, anyway. I knew I was destined to wear the armor and wield the sword.

Unity. True unity in Christ, camaraderie in the mountain, the feasts and celebrations; these are the features of the kingdom of heaven. There is no strife, there is no competition, there is no relational pretense, and there is no whisper of deceit. There is only life. There is only joy.

If the kingdom of heaven operated like the world, no one would ever leave the mountain and fight for the sons and daughters of Christ languishing in the slime. In my vision, I didn't want to leave. I wasn't thinking about the people floundering on the outside because I was too enamored by the beauty of the mountain. But that's not the way the kingdom of heaven works.

Today we have an opportunity to experience the kingdom in limited measure, but in the age to come we will walk into the fullness of this magical place. Heaven is a world where we lay down our lives for one another, where we value and esteem one another, and where we share our glory with one another. It's a place where everyone is dazzlingly and magnificently unique, and uniquely loved.

If you are interested in doing away with the status quo that pervades the IDP camp, you're not alone. Start questioning the ingrained wisdom of the camp. Seek counsel with sagacious friends and family, courageously encourage your loved ones, and put the brakes on your life in tent-city. Examine God's destiny for you in the mountain. Don't try to change the world in a day; this journey will take the rest of your life. Let yourself be joined to the principles and the people who align with truth, and by all means, have some fun!

This is not a journey of drudgery. To the extent that hardship exists so does elation. Ours is a kingdom marked by the jubilant, the amusing, the rambunctious, the absurd, and the hilarious. It can get a little taxing when you're shaking off decades-old chains, but once you're free of them everything changes.

The heart that longs still beats with passion from the center of the mountain. To abide in the mountain is our birthright. To experience the joy of freedom is our inheritance. Intimacy is our destiny. To accept or deny the offering is our choice and ours alone.

Once the kingdom populates, Christ will set foot on this dusty rock once again and in that hour He will do away with the vertical hierarchy, the clown, and all the pink establishments of man. He will usher His beloved into a cosmic wedding feast and establish our union in paradise, for eternity.

About the Author

Nathan Schnackenberg is the author of numerous other works including the *Anno Domini Series* and *Pathways to Abandon*. These works are available at www.amazon.com.

Nate lives with his wife and two children in Colorado. To connect with him, or to book a speaking engagement, link with him at the following Internet locations:

www.facebook.com/nathan.schnackenberg
www.nathanschnackenberg.com

www.ingramcontent.com/pod-product-compliance
Lightning Source LLC
Chambersburg PA
CBHW060150050426
42446CB00013B/2752